Stepping Up To

OS/2 2.1

Upgrade from DOS and/or Windows in a hurry

by Robert Albrecht and Michael Plura

Abacus

A Data Becker Book

Copyright © 1993   Abacus
                          5370 52nd Street SE
                          Grand Rapids, MI 49512

Copyright © 1993   Data Becker, GmbH
                          Merowingerstrasse 30
                          4000 Duesseldorf, Germany

Managing Editor	Louise Benzer
Editors	Louise Benzer, Scott Slaughter, Robbin Markley, Al Wier
Technical Editor	Jim D'Haem, Mike Bergsma
Cover Art	John Plummer/Dick Droste

Library of Congress Cataloging-in-Publication Data

Albrecht, Robert M., 1970-
    Stepping up to OS/2 / Robert Albrecht, Michael Plura.
        p. cm.
    Includes index.
    ISBN 1-55755-185-5 : $16.95
    1. Operating systems (Computers) 2. MS OS/2 (Computer file)
I. Plura, Michael, 1965- . II. Title.
QA76.76.063A42 1992   92-25284
005.4'469--dc20   CIP

Printed in U.S.A.

10   9   8   7   6   5   4   3   2   1

Stepping Up To OS/2 2.1

Stepping Up To OS/2 2.1

Contents

1. Installation   1

1.1	Preparing for Installation	1
	Failsafe boot diskette for DOS users	2
	Installation requirements	3
	Installation methods	4
	Multiple partitions and multiple operating systems	6
	HPFS or FAT	7
	Advantages of the HPFS	7
	Summary	8
	Special installation considerations	9
1.2	Starting the Installation	10
1.3	Creating a Partition for OS/2	12
	Creating partitions	15
	Boot Manager	16
	Suggested setup	17
	File System	17
1.4	OS/2 and DOS	18
	Drive selection	20
	Deleting OS/2	21
1.5	Minimal, Complete, and Selective Installation	22
	Minimal installation - Install preselected features	22
	Complete installation - Install all features	23
	Selective installation - Select features and install	23
	System Configuration	24
	Selective Installation - Setup	27
	OS/2 DOS and WIN-OS/2 support	28
	Pull-down menus	30
	Software configuration menu	31
	Install push button	34
	Advanced Options	34

1.6   Printer and Display Setup 37
      Installation Complete 37
      DOS Partition 38
1.7   Migrate Applications 38
1.8   CONFIG.SYS 40

2. High Performance File System   41

2.1   Filenames..42
2.2   Extended Attributes...44
2.3   Caching..46
2.4   How HPFS Operates 48
      HPFS Original Design..48
      Saving space 48
      Speed...49

3. Workplace Shell   51

3.1   Startup Screen 52
3.2   Object Menu..53
3.3   Setting Up the Workplace Shell.......................................55
3.4   Working with Objects..59
      Opening an object 59
      Selecting objects...60
      Copying and moving objects...60
      Deleting objects...61
      Printing objects...62
      Shadow objects 62
      Renaming objects...64
3.5   Drive Windows...65
      Opening drive windows...65
      Searching for files 66
      Formatting diskettes...67
      Checking diskettes 68
      Changing the sorting sequence..69
      Arranging icons...70
      Free disk space..70
      Changing partitions..70
3.6   Program Groups Are No Longer Necessary.......................71
3.7   Settings 73
      Programs...75
      Directories..78
      Desktop 82
      Data object 83

3.8 Shredder...83
3.9 Templates...84
Templates folder...84
Using Templates..84
Creating templates...85
Deleting templates...88
Associations between objects...............................88
3.10 Command Line..88
Command Prompts...88
Status line...89
HELP...89
Compatibility..90
Ending a session...90

4. Help in OS/2 2.1   91

4.1 Tutorial...92
4.2 Start Here...92
Search...93
Printing...93
4.3 Command Reference..94
Finding Information..94
Storing...95
Bookmark...96
4.4 REXX Information...96
4.5 Master Help Index...97
4.6 Glossary...98

5. DOS Windows   99

5.1 Launching Programs...99
5.2 Setting Up Programs..100
5.3 Settings...100
DOS Settings..102
5.4 Memory Management...111
5.5 CONFIG.SYS..112
5.6 AUTOEXEC.BAT..113
5.7 Booting a DOS Window...113
Starting a window..113
Exiting...113
Configuring DOS..113
Image file...114
5.8 Device Drivers...115

6. Using Windows Programs — 117

6.1   Setting Up Programs 118
6.2   Launching Programs 118
6.3   Settings 119
        WIN_RUNMODE 119
        WIN_DDE 119
        WIN_CLIPBOARD 119
6.4   Windows Device Drivers 120

7. Multitasking and File Swapping — 121

7.1   Multitasking Basics 121
7.2   Launching Several Programs 122
7.3   A Multitasking Practice Lesson 123
7.4   File Swapping 124
        DDE 124

8. System Setup — 125

8.1   Mouse 125
8.2   Sound 126
8.3   System 127
8.4   Country 130
8.5   Font Palette 131
8.6   Colors 131
8.7   Spooler 133
8.8   Keyboard 134
        Keyboard timings 134
8.9   System Clock 135
        Setting the alarm 135
        Setting the system date and clock time 135
8.10 WIN-OS/2 Setup 136
        Dynamic Data Exchange 136
        Clipboard 136

9. Printing Under OS/2 2.1 — 137

9.1   Printer Installation 137
9.2   Spooler 138
9.3   Printing from DOS Windows and Windows 139
9.4   Making Hardcopies 139

10. Productivity Folder   141

10.1   PM Diary..141
        Activities List..142
        Alarms...142
        Calculator 143
        Calendar..144
        Daily Planner...144
        Database..145
        Monthly Planner...145
        Note Pad..145
        Planner Archive 146
        Spreadsheet 146
        Sticky Pad 147
        To Do list 148
        To Do List Archive 148
        Tune Editor 148
10.2   Icon Editor...148
        Using the Icon Editor..148
        Options 151
        Changing colors..152
        Additional functions 153
        Creating a new icon 153
10.3   OS/2 System Editor 153
        Block operations 154
        Search and Replace 155
        Color 156
10.4   Enhanced Editor...156
        Using the Enhanced Editor..157
        Default settings..160
        Editor commands 161
10.5   PM Chart 162
        Tool Bar...163
        Block operations 165
        Creating a diagram..166
        Additional settings 166
10.6   PM Terminal...167
10.7   Pulse 168
10.8   Seek and Scan Files..168
        Working with the list..170
        Options 170

11. OS/2 2.1 Games   171

11.1   Chess...171
11.2   Jigsaw..172
11.3   Cat and Mouse...172
11.4   Scramble...173
11.5   Reversi..173
11.6   Klondike..173

12. Batch Files And REXX   175

12.1   REXX Basics...176
12.2   Writing Programs..176
12.3   Launching Programs..179

Appendix A Tips For Using OS/2   181

Appendix B Command Reference   183

Index   253

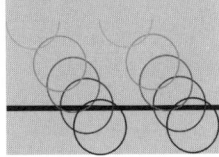

Stepping Up To OS/2 2.1

——— Preface ———

IBM actually did it, OS/2 2.1 is a real product. We congratulate the developers in Boca Raton. Long before IBM's announcement, a number of tremendous features were already being attributed to OS/2 2.1. When IBM made its official announcement, OS/2 sounded too good to be true.

However, IBM kept its promises. OS/2 2.1 is a solid, quick, powerful, reliable operating system. It also gives users the option of running DOS, Windows and OS/2 applications, all at the same time. In other words, it's a truly integrated platform.

From a technical standpoint, the system is absolutely irresistible. It offers full memory protection and solid multitasking. It's also stable in networks and offers a highly consistent user interface. In addition, OS/2 is easier to program, because it works with a linear memory model and has a well defined user interface.

For once the advertising claim:

A Better DOS than DOS and a better Windows than Windows

is more than an advertising claim, it's the truth.

This book is meant for users who are already familiar with DOS and Windows and would like to *step-up* to OS/2 2.1. We won't cover every detail of OS/2 2.1, that would be beyond the scope of this book. We will give DOS and Windows users a brief overview of OS/2 2.1 features and benefits and show them how they can painlessly step-up to OS/2 2.1.

We have marked the most important paragraphs with the following icons:

NOTE   This is the *Note* icon. Paragraphs with this icon contain important notes, make sure to read these paragraphs.

WARNING   This is the *Warning* icon. Paragraphs with this icon contain important warnings that will help you avoid any pitfalls or disasters.

Robert M. Albrecht and Michael Plura

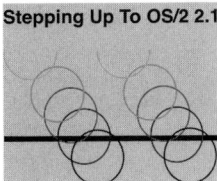

Chapter 1

—— **Installation** ——

In this chapter we'll help you install OS/2. As you can imagine, installing a comprehensive multitasking system such as OS/2 is very complicated. However, once you use OS/2 and experience its dependability and user-friendliness, you'll realize it's worth the effort.

To simplify working with OS/2, first you must transfer it from the diskettes to the hard drive of your system. This is similar to installing DOS or Windows, for example. The installation process will take approximately an hour and a half, depending on your computer.

1.1   Preparing for Installation

Before installing OS/2, you must consider several points. The information in the following sections will help you install OS/2 properly and optimally.

Backup copies of the original diskettes

You should never install software from the original diskettes because some installation programs, for example, write data to g17

these diskettes during the installation process. Also, programming errors or other problems could destroy the original diskettes.

So, for safety reasons, make copies of your original OS/2 installation diskettes. Use one of the many Public Domain or Shareware copying programs or use the DOS utility program:

```
DISKCOPY A: A:
```

Once you've copied the diskettes, store the originals in a safe place for later use. If you decide not to copy all the diskettes, make sure to copy the first three installation diskettes and keep them near your computer.

Backing up the hard drive

You should backup your hard drive, especially if it contains important data that would be difficult to replace. Although making a backup copy of your hard drive may be tedious work, it's a very important task. Otherwise, you may lose important data if your hard drive is suddenly erased.

Installing OS/2 provides an opportunity to clean up your hard drive and store the data on a backup. OS/2 allows you to have both a DOS and a HPFS file system on your hard drive. Then you can use the new OS/2 HPFS (High Performance File System, see Chapter 2) and install a boot manager that will let you choose which drive to boot each time you start the system.

WARNING

> **Be Careful Changing Data**
>
> When you change the partition data on your hard drive (whether in DOS or OS/2), the slightest error can cause complete loss of data.

Failsafe boot diskette for DOS users

Installing new software may lead to problems which can be difficult to diagnose. You're taking a risk anytime you or a program modifies your CONFIG.SYS or AUTOEXEC.BAT.

Therefore, we recommend DOS users create a "Failsafe" boot diskette. A Failsafe boot diskette contains essential files to get your computer running again. It's simply a bootable floppy diskette containing system files, such as COMMAND.COM, and the CONFIG.SYS and AUTOEXEC.BAT files.

A Failsafe boot diskette guarantees that in all but the most extreme circumstances, you can recover from most system problems. If your computer won't boot, insert the Failsafe boot disk, reboot, then copy the necessary files back onto your hard disk. (You should write protect your Failsafe boot diskette and store it in a safe place after you create it.)

Creating a Failsafe boot diskette is easy. Just follow these simple step by step instructions before making any software or operating system modifications to your PC.

1. Purchase diskettes specifically for your disk drive. If you have a 1.4 Meg drive for drive A:, buy some 1.4 Meg high-density diskettes; if you have a 1.2 Meg drive, buy some 1.2 Meg high-density diskettes; and so on.

2. Start your computer and wait until the DOS system prompt appears, for example:

    ```
    C:\>
    ```

3. Insert one of the diskettes you purchased in drive A:.

4. Type FORMAT A:/S (Enter). The /S switch will transfer the system to the diskette.

5. When the command asks you to insert a diskette, press (Enter) (you already inserted one in step 3).

6. FORMAT will prompt you for a "volume label". Type FAILSAFE (Enter).

7. FORMAT will ask if you want to format another diskette. Type N (Enter).

8. When the system prompt appears, type COPY C:\AUTOEXEC.BAT A:(Enter).

9. When the system prompt appears, type COPY C:*.SYS A:(Enter).

10. When the system prompt appears, type CD C:\DOS (Enter). Be sure to use the correct path (in our example, C:\DOS\) for your system.

11. When the system prompt appears, type COPY FORMAT*.* A:(Enter).

12. When the system prompt appears, type COPY UN*.* A:(Enter).

13. Place a write protect tab on the diskette (5.25") or open the write protect (3.5").

14. Edit the AUTOEXEC.BAT and CONFIG.SYS files to load the necessary files from drive A:. Insert the diskette in drive A: to test if it boots properly.

15. Keep this diskette in a safe place in case something goes wrong with your software changes and you have to reboot.

Installation requirements

You must have a 386 or a 486 if you want to install OS/2 2.1. The older 286's accept only the old OS/2 version (1.3). XT users cannot use OS/2 at all.

Avoid using OS/2 on a 386SX because OS/2 2.1 is a 32-bit operating
system and this 386SX processor works externally with only 16
bits. Although this doesn't affect Windows, for example, it would
significantly decrease the operating speed of OS/2 2.1.

Since the 486SX is actually a 486 without a math coprocessor, you
should use a faster 386 instead. OS/2 2.1 requires at least 4 Meg of
RAM. OS/2 2.1 will use all available memory and then uses space
on the hard drive as virtual memory, which causes the entire
system to slow down.

The ideal minimum amount of RAM is 8 Meg because it results in a
noticeable increase in speed. Obviously, additional RAM will
increase speed correspondingly, but isn't necessary for normal use.

Because OS/2 2.1 has a graphical user interface (GUI), you'll need
a graphics card, which supports CGA, Hercules, PS/2 Display
Adapter, XGA, 8514/A, or VGA. Drivers supplied by specific card
manufacturers can access other graphics cards.

HINT

Since OS/2 works well with a mouse, you should use one
if possible.

Your computer should also have a hard drive. The faster and
bigger the hard drive, the better. A hard drive with 40 Meg with
an average speed of 28 milliseconds (ms) or less is the minimum
that's acceptable.

OS/2 occupies at least 20 Meg for a minimal installation. This
type of installation doesn't include DOS or Windows support.
However, these two features are what make OS/2 so unique. So,
for a complete installation, you'll need at least 32 Meg of free
space on the hard drive.

Actually, you should have 50 to 60 Meg available if you want a lot
of room to do your work. Of course there are no upper limits to the
amount of space than can be made available for OS/2.

Installation methods

Dual boot

There are two ways to install OS/2. One method is called the
Dual boot method which installs OS/2 on your DOS formatted
hard disk. With this method, you install OS/2 in a DOS system
that's already set up on drive C:. So, OS/2 and DOS coexist on the
hard drive but in different directories.

In this case, you can use a small program (BOOT.COM) to switch between the systems, but you must reboot each time you switch between the DOS and OS/2 systems.

DOS and OS/2 together

You can install OS/2, in addition to your existing DOS, on the C: drive, similar to installing Windows. You can locate the operating system in an OS/2 subdirectory. With the help of a small program, you can then boot either DOS or OS/2. (Unlike Windows, OS/2 is a complete operating system instead of only a graphic operating system expansion.)

So, if you're working under DOS and want to boot OS/2, you simply type:

```
BOOT /OS2
```

Notice the /OS2 switch, this is the correct syntax; BOOT OS/2 is an incorrect syntax for the command. The computer then automatically copies several system files, starts again, and boots OS/2. You can switch back to the DOS boot in a similar way by typing the same command but with a different parameter:

```
BOOT /DOS
```

This type of installation is called *Dual boot*. Use this method if you're not sure about installing OS/2.

To do this, you must make sure that the following statements are in your DOS configuration files:

In CONFIG.SYS:

```
SHELL = C:\DOS\COMMAND.COM /P
```

In the AUTOEXEC.BAT:

```
SET COMSPEC=C:\DOS\COMMAND.COM
```

HINT

Be sure to use the correct path (in our example, C:\DOS\) for your system.

By using this method, you can continue to use your computer as you always have and you can easily delete OS/2 off the hard drive by erasing all OS/2 directories. Unfortunately, the disadvantage of this method is that you must continue to use the existing DOS FAT file system. OS/2 normally works with a HPFS (High

Performance File System), which offers several advantages over the FAT (File Allocation Table) file system that's used in DOS.

Basic Installation

The second method of installing OS/2 is called the *Basic Installation*. This involves creating a separate partition just for OS/2 (this may even be the old DOS partition) and formatting it with the HPFS (High Performance File System). Remember, this will delete all existing data on the drive.

Once you've formatted a partition with the HPFS, you can't access this partition when you boot DOS. But when you open a DOS Window under OS/2, you can access the partition as you would any other drive.

HINT

> If you want to work with OS/2 briefly, use the Dual boot method. But if you want to work with OS/2 extensively and use the OS/2 applications, use the Basic Installation method.

Multiple partitions and multiple operating systems

The hard drive is divided into sections, called partitions. So, one large partition can occupy the entire hard drive or several small partitions can occupy the available space on the drive. A partition can be a *primary* partition or a *logical* partition.

Each primary partition can contain a different operating system (e.g., DOS, OS/2, or UNIX) or file system (e.g., HPFS or FAT). Only one primary partition can be active at any time. You can boot the system (start the operating system) from any primary partition. OS\2 also allows you to boot from logical partitions.

DOS and OS/2 make it possible to further divide any partition. This creates several logical drives under DOS (D:, E:, F:,...).

OS/2 includes an easy to use partition editor (FDISK) and a Boot Manager that will help you set up a flexible system, which can boot DOS, OS/2 or another operating system. OS/2's Boot Manager is equivalent to a small 1 Meg partition that displays a small menu. From this menu you can easily select another partition, from which the current operating system can be booted. So, the Boot Manager switches between several bootable partitions.

Using FDISK it's possible to set up a small primary DOS partition (of about 10 Meg) and a sufficiently large OS/2 partition (of at least 40 Meg) and insert them into the Boot Manager menu. Then you can boot DOS or OS/2. You can also set up a logical DOS FAT partition and then install the DOS applications, tools, etc., in the logical DOS FAT partition. Once you do this, you'll be able to access all your files and data in the logical DOS FAT from OS/2 and DOS.

HPFS or FAT

Regardless of whether you want to install OS/2 on a newly partitioned hard drive or into an existing partition, you must decide which file system to use.

Disadvantages of typical DOS FAT file systems

The FAT (File Allocation Table) file system, which is used by all versions of DOS for file management, was designed to manage smaller files on 160K diskettes. So, this system is suitable for media with small storage capacities.

Since today's hard drives start at 80 Meg, an OS/2 system should include a hard drive with at least a 200 Meg capacity. Compared to the old 160K diskettes, this is already more than 1,000 times the capacity.

Even the size of individual files has reached megabyte capacity. So, the old FAT file system is no longer adequate for such large files. The files have increased so much that the FAT file manager can no longer manage them. Therefore, using the FAT file system under OS/2 in partitions larger than 50 to 60 Meg results in loss of speed.

Advantages of the HPFS

The HPFS (High Performance File System) is designed for today's generation of computers. Larger amounts of data can be managed on bigger hard drives.

Longer, more meaningful filenames

The HPFS provides more freedom in selecting filenames. Now filenames can have a maximum of 254 characters and can even include several periods and spaces. Also, under OS/2 you can assign several attributes to these files.

Freely definable attributes

With HPFS you can assign any number of attributes to every file under OS/2. While you can assign or remove a maximum of eight existing attributes (by inserting or deleting a special bit), under

HPFS you can create your own attributes and assign these any character chains you want. For example:

```
VirusCheckSum=3672
Operation_ by=Meier_two
Created_by=Turbo_Pascal_6
```

In this way, you could easily create a virus scanner (anti-virus program) that runs permanently in the background (multitasking), calculates check sums of files, and compares these with stored files in an expanded data attribute.

OS/2 also "remembers" certain information, such as the dates files were created, the date of the last access, and how many times the files were accessed.

Less fragmentation

Whenever you store a file of only one byte, under normal circumstances, a DOS formatted hard drive will use two kilobytes (2048 bytes). This is because the FAT divides the space on the hard drive into clusters of two kilobytes. Larger hard drives have clusters of 4, 8, or 16K. However, the HPFS uses sectors of 512 bytes. So, you can store more data on an HPFS partition than on a FAT partition of the same size.

Summary

You should select HPFS during basic installation for the OS/2 2.1 partition. HPFS is a high performance file system that meets today's needs and noticeably increases the speed of OS/2. Also, you don't have to use the limited filenames of the FAT file system, which can have only eight characters and a three character extension.

File System Comparison		
	FAT	HPFS
Max. partition size	128-2048 Meg	2,097,153 Meg(=2.048 Giga)
Max. file size	2 Giga	2048 Giga
Length of filename	8+3 characters	254 characters
Attributes	8 bit	character chains

You must use genuine OS/2 applications to use the advantages of HPFS. For example, Windows and DOS applications cannot process the long filenames of the HPFS. In this case, OS/2 shortens the filenames when you copy them from the desktop to a FAT partition or a diskette.

HINT

> We recommend that you partition your hard drive into four partitions: two primary partitions, one for DOS and one for OS/2 2.1; one logical FAT partition, accessible from both DOS and OS/2 2.1; and one partition for the Boot Manager.

Special installation considerations

The following are some other features and considerations that can ensure a smooth installation of OS/2 2.1.

VGA cards and the IRQ2

Most VGA cards have a jumper which allows you to set the IRQ to "enabled" or "disabled". In the "enabled" position (which is rare), the jumper setting can cause display errors when switching between various DOS Windows. So, you should set the jumper on your VGA card to "disable". To determine the location and position of the jumper, refer to your computer manual.

VGA cards and Autodetect

If your VGA card has an autodetect switch, you may have to deactivate it before you install OS/2.

Preparing to place DOS and OS/2 on one partition

To operate DOS and OS/2 from the same partition, you will have to set the system variables SHELL and COMSPEC. Make sure that the following line is in your CONFIG.SYS file:

```
SHELL=C:\DOS\COMMAND.COM /P
```

Make sure that the following line is in your AUTOEXEC.BAT file:

```
SET COMSPEC=C:\DOS\COMMAND.COM
```

You must adjust the search path to match the directory structure on your hard drive.

If these lines are not in your CONFIG.SYS and AUTOEXEC.BAT files and you install OS/2 2.1 using the *dual boot* method, you will not be able to boot DOS from OS/2 2.1.

1.2   Starting the Installation

In this section we'll take you step-by-step through the installation process. This section should help you if you encounter any problems.

Now let's begin:

You've finished making a backup of the hard drive and have made a DOS "failsafe boot diskette" containing the most important utility files required to boot your computer.

To begin the actual installation, insert the first diskette, the OS/2 2.1 Installation diskette, in drive A:. Then press either the Reset button or Ctrl + Alt + Del or switch off the computer completely and turn it back on.

The computer now boots from the OS/2 diskette in drive A:.

HINT

> Switch the computer off, wait 30 seconds and switch it on again if nothing happens.

In most BIOS variations, the first 12 characters of the BIOS statement in the upper-left corner of the screen disappear when the computer starts to boot. This is normal and indicates that OS/2 has started booting.

As the installation continues, it may seem like the computer has crashed. However, the installation of OS/2 involves some very complicated processes so it does take some time, be patient.

After awhile, you'll see a large white IBM logo on a blue background and hear a beep. A prompt also appears which asks you to insert the diskette labeled "Operating System/2 Diskette 1" into the floppy drive. OS/2 has now partially booted. The diskette labeled "OS/2 Diskette 1" completes the boot up and the actual installation can begin.

During the first part of the installation you use diskettes 1 to 5. OS/2 will then boot from the hard drive and request the remaining diskettes sequentially.

Insert the diskette labeled "OS/2 Diskette 1" into the drive and press Enter. Now the screen switches to graphic mode and the OS/2 logo appears, along with some copyright warnings. When these messages disappear, the message "Loading, please wait..." is displayed.

This process may also take a long time. However, if nothing happens for about 5 minutes, the system has probably crashed. In this case, press the Reset button and start the installation again.

After the program has been loading for awhile, the greeting page of OS/2 appears. Several additional instructions for using the installation program follow. Press (Enter) at any time to move to the next screen.

By pressing the (Esc) key, you can cancel the installation and access the OS/2 command line. This is useful if you're having problems with the installation. If you exit to the OS/2 command line, typing EXIT will return you to the installation program.

Although you're operating under OS/2, your computer will behave as if you booted DOS from a diskette. If there are problems on the hard drive, you can now start FDISK.COM from the diskette labeled "OS/2 Diskette 1". The CHKDSK.EXE program located on the diskette labeled "OS/2 Diskette 2" can be useful if you experience hard drive errors while booting OS/2.

The last screen explains how to make selections from a list. Then the installation briefly stops before you see the Installation Drive Selection screen.

Partitioning the hard drive with FDISK

Now you must decide whether you want to maintain the existing configuration of your hard drive (*1. Accept the Drive*) or to re-partition the hard drive.

Dual Boot

Accept the drive (*1. Accept the Drive*) if the C: drive has enough space (more than 20 Meg) and you want to add OS/2 to the DOS already present in C: (Dual Boot).

Dual boot installation users should skip the following section and refer to Section 1.4, OS/2 and DOS.

Basic Installation

To install OS/2 2.1 on a separate partition that hasn't been created yet, and perhaps include a Boot Manager, select the second menu item *2. Specify a different drive or partition* which loads the FDISK program of OS/2.

The installation program will suggest that you define the entire drive as C: partition, if your hard drive doesn't have any partitions. Then you can choose between *Accept predefined*

Installation partition (one big C: partition) and *Specify your own Installation partition* (you create the partitions yourself with FDISK).

1.3   Creating a Partition for OS/2

If you select the second menu item and confirm it by pressing Enter, an orange warning screen appears explaining the consequences of changing partitions.

WARNING

> **Back Up Your Hard Drive**
>
> At this point, any errors could cause a complete loss of data. So, be sure that you've backed up your hard drive. Doing this is a lot easier than re-entering all the data and new configurations for every program.

Changes made in the partition chart won't be written to the hard drive until you exit the partition editor, FDISK.COM (Save and Exit). After a brief pause, OS/2 loads the FDISK program and displays the partition data.

If you've ever worked with the FDISK program in a DOS version, you'll notice a few changes. Information about the existing partitions on your hard drive is displayed in the form of a chart. There are five columns on the screen, with different statements about the existing partitions. In the upper-left you'll see a number for each hard drive that FDISK recognized. To switch between the drives, first press Tab and then select the drive by using the → and ← keys.

To select a partition, use the ↓ and ↑ keys. Use the PgUp and End keys to jump to the beginning or end of the list. When you press Enter, you'll see the *Options* menu. Here you can access or erase the various partitions. You can also change their status or insert partitions in the Boot Manager menu.

The individual entries for the partitions have the following meanings:

Name

Under OS/2 you can assign a name, which can contain up to eight characters, to each partition. This should indicate the contents of each partition. These names also appear later in the Boot Manager menu where, for example, you can use the cursor keys to select MS-DOS 6.0, DR DOS 6.0, UNIX, or even OS/2 2.1 and boot with it.

You can give each partition a name (except for the Boot Manager) by selecting *Add to Boot Manager Menu* from the *Options* menu. Its name then appears in the Boot Manager menu and you can select and boot the corresponding partition.

To change a defined name, you must select *Change Partition Name* from the *Options* menu.

Status

You can assign a status to each partition:

None	Usually this refers to logical drives that don't have any of the following three attributes.
Bootable	Partitions with this status appear in the Boot Manager menu and can be launched from there.
Startable	This partition is started first. Usually this should be the Boot Manager, so that you can boot the other partitions from it. If you have assigned the startable status to partitions other than the Boot Manager, they will be launched automatically the next time the system starts. In DOS this status is known as the "active" partition.
Installable	During installation, OS/2 will be installed in the partition with this status. You must assign the status Installable to one partition so the installation can continue.

Access

This indicates whether, when, and how to access a current partition. If possible, your FDISK already displays the drive letters, under which you can access the partitions under DOS or OS/2.

A partition that hasn't been formatted cannot have a drive letter. So the drive letters may shift if you format a partition that's located between two already formatted partitions.

You can boot primary partitions. In the expanded logical partitions, you'll find logical drives. These drives are actually smaller sections of an expanded partition.

Pri/Log	Here you can choose to work with a primary or a logical partition.
Primary	This is a primary partition, from which you can boot.
Logical	This is a logical partition that can contain several logical drives. This type of partition is accessible from both OS/2 and DOS.

FS Type (File System)

Here you can determine whether a partition has already been formatted and what file system performed the formatting. Areas on the hard drive that haven't been assigned a partition are marked *Free Space*.

Free Space	This area on the hard drive hasn't been assigned a partition yet and is therefore available for use.
Unusable	This is a section of the hard drive that cannot be used because your partitioning has left a gap between partitions. You must delete one of the adjacent partitions and use the contiguous area that forms one large partition.
Unformatted	Although this partition has already been created, it hasn't been formatted yet.
FAT	This partition has been formatted with the FAT file system. Even when you boot DOS from a diskette, you have access to this partition.
HPFS	This partition has been formatted with HPFS. You can access this partition only under OS/2. It's also possible to access this partition when you open a DOS Window under OS/2 or when you boot DOS from a diskette under OS/2.

> *BOOT MANAGER*
>> This special partition, which is always exactly one Meg, contains the Boot Manager. With the Boot Manager's menu you can boot other primary partitions.

Megabytes

This allows FDISK to display the size of a partition in megabytes. One Meg corresponds to about 500 pages of type.

Creating partitions

Use the ⬆ and ⬇ keys to select a partition and press Enter. You'll see the *Options* menu. Now you can decide how to use the selected partition.

You can create a new partition when you activate the *Options* menu (press Enter) on a section of the hard drive that's still free (Free Space). To do this, use *Create Partition...*. You can delete any partition with *Delete Partition*.

WARNING

Be Careful Deleting Partitions

Warning prompts won't appear when you delete a partition. Once a partition has been deleted, the data that was stored in the partition cannot be restored.

However, if you made an error, you can abort FDISK (exit without saving) by pressing F3, without causing any damage.

As long as you haven't ended FDISK yet, the disk won't perform any operations. Changes are saved on the hard drive only when you end FDISK with F3 and *Save and Exit*.

During partitioning, remember that you can create only four partitions per hard drive. A primary partition is one, the Boot Manager is a partition, and all logical drives together form one partition (as long as these logical drives are all adjacent). This means that if you want to use the Boot Manager, you can set up three additional partitions. So you can boot three different operating systems, for example.

For each hard drive you can set up only one expanded partition. This partition can naturally hold several logical drives (D:, E:, F:, etc.). You must set up these logical drives sequentially; a primary partition cannot be located between them.

HINT

> You can access the logical drives under OS/2 as well as under DOS if they have been formatted with the FAT file system.

You create a partition, as we previously explained, by selecting *Create partition* from the *Options* menu. A small dialog box asks you for the exact size of the partition. FDISK always suggests the maximum possible size.

At this point, you may also indicate the desired size in megabytes. If the size you indicate is smaller than the amount of space still available, a series of questions, asking you to determine whether the partition should be placed at the beginning or at the end of the free space, appear.

In this way, you can locate, for example, the Boot Manager at the very end of the hard drive. The Boot Manager is in use only when the system starts and can be safely stored at the far end of the hard drive.

Boot Manager

The first choice in the *Options* menu, *Install Boot Manager*, reserves a 1 Meg partition, which contains the Boot Manager itself. By selecting *Add to Boot Manager*, you can add individual partitions to the Boot Manager menu and by selecting *Remove from Boot manager*, you can eliminate these partitions again. By selecting *Change Partition Name*, you can rename the partition.

Under *Set Startup Values* you can determine:

Default	Which partition to boot if you encounter no choices.
Timer	Whether to boot automatically after a certain time interval.
Timeout	How long to wait to boot a partition set under *Default*.
Mode	Whether to display only the filenames or additional data in the Boot Manager. The additional data is the type of partition, file system type and accessibility.

Suggested setup

Our suggested setup is as follows:

Install the Boot Manager first (at the end of the hard drive), followed by a primary OS/2 partition (of at least 50 Meg), a primary DOS partition (of at least 10 Meg), and finally a logical drive (of any remaining Meg) in a further partition.

The Boot Manager partition allows you to boot DOS or OS/2 2.1. Make the Boot Manager the *Startable* partition.

You will have to reformat the primary DOS partition and reinstall DOS, after you have finished the OS/2 2.1 installation. Make the DOS partition *Bootable* and format it later with a *FAT* file system.

Make sure to set the OS/2 primary partitions as *Installable*, so you can complete the installation process and install OS/2. Use the *HPFS* on this partition.

Set the logical partition to *None* so this partition will be accessible from both OS/2 and DOS. Later you can format this partition with a *FAT* file system so it is accessible from both DOS and OS/2.

With this setup it's possible for you to boot either OS/2 (HPFS) or DOS (FAT) and then have access all of your programs and data, as long as the logical drive is formatted with the FAT file system (FAT file system, Drive D:, E:, F:,...).

Once you've entered all your preferences, exit FDISK with F3 and *Save and Exit*. Each time you create new partitions or change the drive names, you must restart the system. To do this, insert the Installation diskette into drive A: and press Enter.

File system

After the disk partitioning is complete, the installation process starts again. You can continue the installation only when the changes to the partitions are complete.

Select the *Accept the drive* option to install OS/2 on the Installable partition you created. Insert Diskette 2 and press Enter.

From the *Select the File System* screen you can decide whether to format the newly created partition with HPFS or the FAT file system. At this point, select the HPFS if possible because OS/2 is designed to work best with this file system.

Formatting takes a few minutes, depending on the computer and the size of the partition.

After the formatting is complete, the Installation program asks for diskettes 3, 4, 5, and then once more, for the Installation diskette.

```
The hard drive preparation is complete. The next step
will be Os/2 system configuration.

Remove the diskette from the diskette drive.

Press the Enter key to start OS/2 system configuration.
_____

The following trademarks are used in this installation
program:

Os/2, Operating System/w, Presentation Manager,
Proprinter, PS/2, Personal System/.w, and
Quitewriter--trademarks of the IBM Corporation.

Microsoft, Microsoft Mouse, and Windows--trademarks
of Microsoft Corporation.

Visi-On--a trademark of VisiCorp>
```

Hard drive preparation completed

Remove the Installation diskette from the drive and press `Enter`. Then your computer reboots from the hard drive.

Skip ahead to Section 1.5, Minimal, Complete, and Selective Installation to complete the OS/2 basic installation process.

1.4   OS/2 and DOS

In this chapter, we'll describe how to install OS/2 in addition to an existing DOS on a shared C: drive. This process won't delete any files or format a disk.

HINT

> To fully use all the advantages of OS/2's capabilities (HPFS, long file names, etc.), don't use this installation procedure. Instead, use the procedure explained in Section 1.3. You may wish to use the dual boot procedure to test OS/2.

Adding OS/2 to an existing DOS in a DOS partition means that this partition must have at least 20 Meg free. However, more space than this should be available because DOS or Windows support is not available with the minimum installation.

You'll probably need about 32 Meg of disk space for a complete installation. To make some extra space for stored files and some data, 40-50 Meg is suitable. Remember that you should have as much space as possible available.

OS/2 knows when you don't have enough free space on your hard drive and will ask you whether you want to continue the installation. In this instance, it would be useless to continue; so you should cancel the installation process by pressing F3. If you continue the installation process, this would result in a full hard drive and the installation process would end with an error. Then booting from the hard drive would be impossible.

HINT

> For this type of installation, the "SHELL=" statement must be in the CONFIG.SYS and the COMSPEC= statement must be in the AUTOEXEC.BAT.

If this isn't the case, before starting the installation, add a line in the CONFIG.SYS as follows:

```
SHELL=C:\DOS\COMMAND.COM /P
```

Add the following line to the AUTOEXEC.BAT:

```
SET COMSPEC=C:\DOS\COMMAND.COM
```

HINT

> Be sure to use the correct path (in our example, C:\DOS\) for your system.

However, before you begin this installation, you must type:

```
CHKDSK C: /F
```

to examine the C: drive for errors in the File Allocation Table. If there are file allocation errors, they could cause data mix-up or data loss during installation.

To prevent such disasters, you should defragment your hard drive by using a utility, such as Norton's SPEEDISK or PC Tools' COMPRESS.

File fragmentation

Whenever you want to store a file, DOS searches the hard drive for the first available empty space. DOS writes to this space until it's full. Then it continues to write in the next available empty space, etc.

Therefore all files are divided among the individual tracks and sectors on the hard drive. When a file must be read, the read/write head of the hard drive tries to access the data.

Since the data isn't located in one sector, the read/write head must continually move to locate the data. This process can slow down data access considerably and eventually damage the read/write head. This is called file fragmentation. This fragmentation is a characteristic of FAT file systems, and no longer exists in HPFS (specifically HPFS386).

Drive selection

After you begin the installation process according to the procedure described in Section 1.2, Starting the Installation, you'll reach the *Installation Drive Selection* window.

The Installation program usually recommends installing OS/2 on drive C:. Accept this recommendation by pressing (Enter) while Option 1, *Accept the drive*, is active. Then the installation program asks for diskette 2. The *Formatting the Installation partition* window appears in a short time.

WARNING

If you select the second option (*Format the partition*), drive C: is formatted and can choose between HPFS and the FAT file system. **However, all data on drive C: will be lost.**

So for now press (1) or (Enter) to select 1. *Do not format the partition.*

WARNING

The program displays a warning if the configuration files don't contain the SHELL= and SET COMSPEC= statements. If this occurs, cancel the installation and modify the configuration files using an ASCII editor (EDIT) before returning to the installation.

Otherwise, you can wait and modify these files under OS/2 with the OS/2 Systems Editor. Make sure that you modify the AUTOEXEC.BAT and CONFIG.SYS files before you try to boot DOS. If you do not modify these files DOS will not boot. If this happens you can use the Failsafe boot diskette, described in the previous section, to boot DOS and then modify these files.

Then the Installation program transfers files from diskette 2 and then asks for diskettes 3, 4, 5, and the Install diskette.

When this hard disk preparation part of the installation is complete, remove the last diskette from the drive and press (Enter) to reboot your computer.

Skip ahead to Section 1.5, Minimal, Complete, and Selective Installation to complete the installation process.

Deleting OS/2

If necessary, you can easily delete OS/2 from the hard drive when you used the dual boot installation process. Simply type the following at the OS/2 command line

```
BOOT /DOS
```

to boot DOS and then delete the OS/2 directories. Since there are several subdirectories, you should use a utility program that deletes complete directories. The XDEL command from DR DOS 6.0 is an example of such a utility:

```
C:
CD \
XDEL DESKTOP /S/D/R
XDEL NOWHERE /S/D/R
XDEL OS2 /S/D/R
XDEL SPOOL /S/D/R
```

This sequence deletes all OS/2 specific directories and their subdirectories. Now you must also delete the OS/2 system files from the root directory:

```
XDEL OS2*.* /R
```

Two hidden system files remain on each drive addressed by OS/2. You cannot locate these files by simply using the DIR command (the expanded attributes are hidden in EA DATA.SF and WP ROOT.SF). You must remove both of these files from each drive with the command:

```
XDEL C:\*.?SF /R
XDEL D:\*.?SF /R
XDEL E:\*.?SF /R
```

Deleting these files from all the drives completely removes OS/2 from the hard drive.

1.5   Minimal, Complete, and Selective Installation

The first part of the installation is now complete. The main portion of OS/2 is on your hard drive. Now OS/2 will boot from the hard drive.

In the next installation step a window is displayed in which you can select the size of OS/2 to install on your hard drive. If you're not familiar with the mouse, you can watch a brief tutorial on using the mouse. As the installation continues, occasionally you must use the mouse to make your selections. To activate this tutorial, simply press (Enter).

HINT

> Windows users should view the mouse tutorial, since OS/2 2.1 uses both mouse buttons in a different way than Windows.

Minimal installation - *Install preselected features*

By selecting *Install preselected features*, the Install program will copy only the kernel of the drive system and a small selection of the most important help programs to the hard drive.

HINT

> If you choose this minimal installation, you can later install the other features under OS/2. To install the other features while running OS/2 enter INSTALL on the command line or from the *System Setup* folder, double-click on the *Selective Install* icon. Now you can install all the features that haven't been installed yet.

The following features won't be installed when you select *Install preselected features*:

- Online Command Reference

- Online Help for REXX

- Any font other than System Proportional and Helvetica

The following utility programs:

- Display directory tree

- Label diskettes

- Link object modules

- Picture viewer

- PMREXX

- Recover files

The following tools and games:

- Enhanced editor

- Terminal emulator

- PM Chart

- Solitaire (Klondike)

- Reversi

- Scramble

- Cat and Mouse

- Pulse

- Jigsaw

- Chess

Also, the additional bitmaps and PCMCIA won't be installed.

You should use this type of installation when there is limited space on the hard drive. This installation requires about 25 Meg of free space. These features can be installed at a later time by typing INSTALL at the OS/2 command prompt.

Complete installation - *Install all features*

The opposite of minimal installation is obviously complete installation. To select this type of installation, activate *Install all features* and click on OK. All features will be copied to the hard drive.

Selective installation - *Select features and install*

With selective installation, you decide what should be installed. Whenever possible, you should choose this method of installation. To do so, activate *Select features and install* and click on OK.

Regardless of the installation method you select, you'll see another window, in which you can assign several specifications for your computer system and country setting.

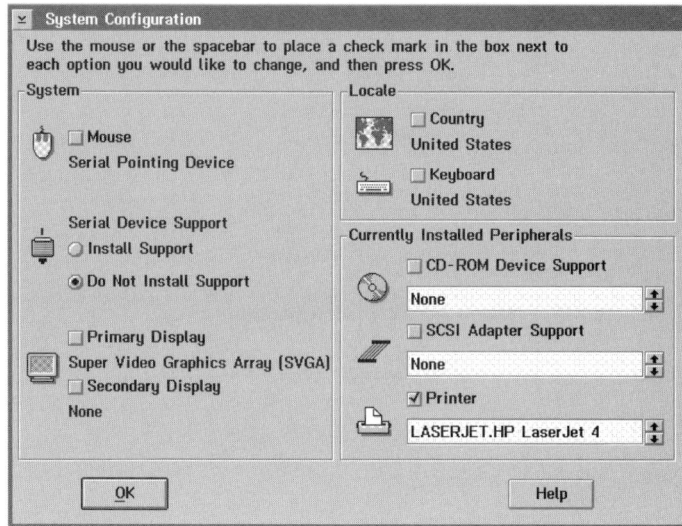

Select your computer's hardware in this window

Activate all the options you want to modify by clicking on them using the mouse. A second click cancels the activation. Finally, click on OK. The System Configuration dialog is displayed.

System configuration

Mouse

You can select the type of mouse you have with the mouse option. If you don't have a mouse, select *No pointing device support*. However, using OS/2 without a mouse can be very tedious.

If your mouse type isn't listed, try using it with the *Serial Pointing Device* setting. Select *Other Pointing Device for Mouse Port*. This generic driver works with almost every mouse. Then you must indicate to which COM port the mouse is connected. Normally, this is COM1 or COM2; it's rare to have this as COM3 or COM4.

Serial Device Support

The *Serial Device Support* option allows you to install support for external modems, plotters and printers attached to your computer using the serial port. A mouse attached to the serial port is configured in the *Mouse* setting window.

Primary display

You can select your graphics card with this option. You can choose from *CGA, EGA, PS/2-VGA, 8514/A, XGA*, and *SVGA*. However, usually the installation program has already made the correct selection.

Select *Other* if you have a special graphics card together with an OS/2 2.1 driver.

Secondary display

If you have two graphics cards in your computer, you can use this option to indicate a second graphics card. In addition to the options for the primary adapter, you can also indicate a Hercules card in the *Secondary Adapter*.

Text mode applications should be executed on the second graphics card, if one is available. Because of this, you should select the higher resolution screen (meaning the one with the better graphics) for your primary graphics adapter.

If you have only one graphics card, select *None*.

Country

This option lets you make any country-specific settings. These include the currency and time and date formats.

Use the *Code Page* option carefully if you select a language other than English. Use the *National* setting because, when you use the DOS windows later, several graphic symbols will not be displayed correctly if *Multilingual* is selected. This would also occur with Norton Commander, among others.

Keyboard

You can indicate the keyboard's layout by using this option. A variety of foreign language keyboards are available. Simply select the keyboard layout for your system in the list when this option is checked.

CD-ROM Device Support

This option allows you to quickly and easily attach a CD-ROM for use in OS/2 2.1. The supported CD-ROM devices include the following:

- Hitachi CDR-1650, 1750, 3650, 3750

- IBM CD-ROM I and II

- NEC CDR-36, 37, 72, 73, 74, 83, 84

- Panasonic CR-501

- LK-MC501S

- Sony CDU-541, 6111, 6211, 7211

- Texcel DM-3021, 5201, 3024, 5024

- Toshiba 3201, 3301

Select *Other* if you have an unlisted CD-ROM with an OS/2 2.1 driver provided by the CD-ROM manufacturer.

SCSI Adapter Support

This option allows you to support a SCSI adapter. SCSI is an acronym for Small Computer System Interface. This interface is gaining wide acceptance as a method of attaching peripherals to a computer.

The supported SCSI adapters include:

- IBM PS/2 SCSI adapters

- Adaptec 1510, 1512, 1520, 1522, 1540, 1542, 1544, 1640, 1642, 1644, 1740, 1742, 1744

- DPT PM2001 and PM2012

- Future Domain 1660, 1670, 1680, 850IBM, 860, 870, 880, 7000EX and MCS 700

Printer

The *Printer* option allows you to specify the printer that is attached to your system. Simply select the correct printer driver from the list. If no printer is selected, then IBMNULL printer is installed.

If your printer does not appear on the list, select a compatible printer. If there isn't a compatible printer driver, try the following:

For 9-pin printers try:

> *Epson 9 pins - 80 columns*

For 24-pin printers try:

> *Epson 24 pins - 80 columns* or *Epson LQ-850 24 pins*

Most printers are compatible with these Epson printers.

Port Setting

You still must indicate to which port the printer is connected. Usually LPT1 is the correct setting. When you've made your selection and click [OK], the Installation program will ask you for the corresponding printer driver diskette.

Continue Installation

Finally, click [OK].

If you've selected either the Minimal or Complete Installation, you can skip the following section because it's needed only for Selective Installation.

Selective installation - Setup

The *OS/2 Setup and Installation* window appears.

A small window, labeled *Disk Space*, appears in the lower-right. This window constantly indicates the space available and the space needed by the current installation on the hard drive.

This enables you to exclude the features you don't need. To do this, click on the appropriate check box to remove a small check mark.

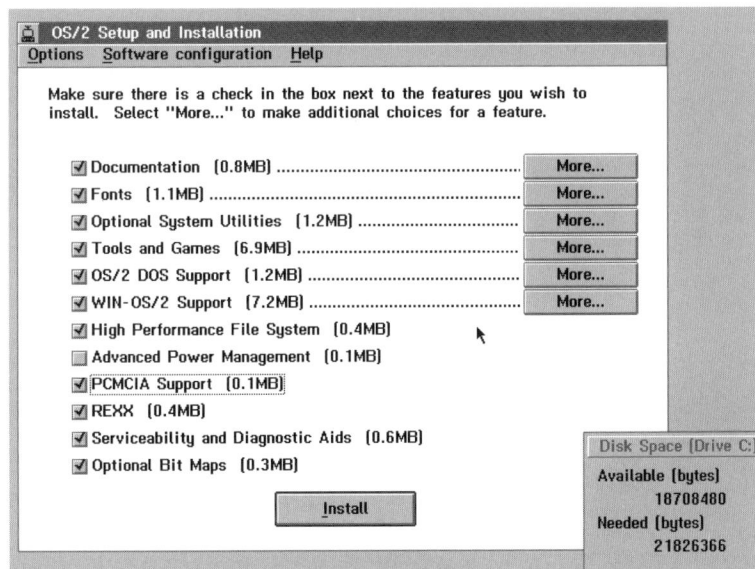

OS/2 Setup and Installation

For some features, you can click on a push button labeled [More...]. When you do this, a window appears in which you can make more precise selections during installation.

Also, this is where you find information about the exact amount of space needed for each individual feature.

You can select the following features:

Documentation

This feature helps you determine what Online Help should be installed. Online Help can be very useful later when you're using OS/2.

The OS/2 *Tutorial* provides a small introduction about how to use OS/2 2.1. This tutorial also helps explain the basic functions and features.

The OS/2 *Command Reference* contains help for all OS/2 commands.

The *REXX Information* provides all the Help settings for the powerful REXX language, with which you can easily write powerful batch files.

Fonts

This is where you select the fonts you want to install. If you deactivate all fonts, only the System Proportional and Helvetica fonts are installed.

Optional System Utilities

From this list, you can select the system utility programs that you want to install.

Tools and Games

You can exclude these utility programs and all the games from the installation to save disk space. The 1.5 Meg Terminal Emulator can be eliminated if you don't have a modem or a null-modem connection to another computer.

If you won't be creating charts, you can also eliminate PM Chart. Personal Productivity contains several smaller programs, such as an alarm clock, a pocket calculator, and a calendar.

OS/2 DOS and WIN-OS/2 support

This allows you to determine the settings for the DOS and Windows environment.

```
┌─────────────────────────────────────────┐
│ ⌄  OS/2 DOS Support                       │
│ ┌─Virtual Memory Management─────────────┐ │
│ │ Make sure there is a check mark next to each │
│ │ item you wish to install.             │ │
│ │                                       │ │
│ │ ☑ DOS Protect Mode Interface [20KB]   │ │
│ │                                       │ │
│ │ ☑ Virtual Expanded Memory Management [18KB] │
│ │                                       │ │
│ │ ☑ Virtual Extended Memory Support [8KB] │ │
│ └───────────────────────────────────────┘ │
│                                           │
│    ┌────────┐ ┌────────┐ ┌────────┐      │
│    │   OK   │ │ Cancel │ │  Help  │      │
│    └────────┘ └────────┘ └────────┘      │
└─────────────────────────────────────────┘
```

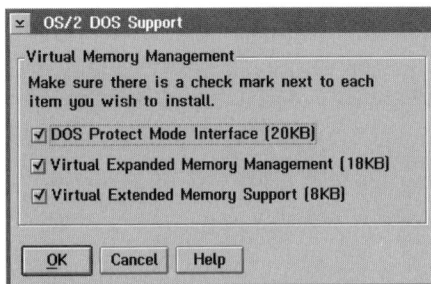

Do I need DOS programs?

The *DOS Protected Mode Interface* is needed if you'll eventually run programs, which support DPMI specifications, in the DOS windows.

If you want to install DOS programs that need EMS support according to the LIM EMS specification, you should leave the *Virtual Expanded Memory Management* option switched on.

This frees up as much as 32 Meg of Expanded Memory (EMS) in a DOS window.

The *Virtual Extended Memory Support* option works in a similar way. You'll have extended memory, according to LIMA XMS specifications, available for DOS windows later, only when these drivers are installed along with the other drivers.

Besides, memory designations, such as High Memory Area (HMA), Extended Memory Blocks (EMB), and Upper Memory Blocks (UMB) are also included.

High Performance File System

The High Performance File System option is only available if you have a hard drive partition formatted with the FAT file system available.

This option allows you to install both the HPFS and the FAT file systems. You must have two partitions available to use both file systems.

Advanced Power Management

Many laptops and notebook computers now include Advanced Power Management facilities which allows them to maximize battery life. Select this option if your computer supports Advanced Power Management.

PCMCIA Support

Many laptops and notebook computers now support cards that follow standards set by PC Memory Card International Association. OS/2 2.1 supports these PCMCIA adapters. Select this option if your system supports these adapters.

REXX

REXX is a procedural batch language for OS/2. It's much more powerful than the DOS batch commands. You should install the REXX language.

Serviceability and Diagnostic Aids

The *Serviceability and Diagnostic Aids* are diagnostic programs used to report any problems that may occur.

Optional Bit Maps

The *Optional Bit Maps* allow you to customize the background of your OS/2 desktop.

Pull-down menus

While running the OS/2 Setup and Installation program, you'll see a pull-down menu under the title bar.

To begin the installation, select *Options/Install* or the [Install] push button. You can also format the hard drive partitions installed with FDISK, if necessary. *Options/Format* displays a window that lists all the accessible hard drive partitions. Click on these to see whether they have already been formatted.

If you want to re-format one of the partitions or format the logical partition you created with FDISK, click on the corresponding drive icon and determine under *Format* whether to format the partition with HPFS (*Format HPFS*) or with the FAT file system (*Format FAT*).

> **HINT**
>
> Select *Format FAT* if you want to format the logical DOS partition so you can access the partition from DOS and OS/2.

This is a good time to assign a volume label, if desired. The hard drive partitions labeled in this way won't be formatted until you click on the [Format] push button.

An OS/2 Command Interpreter is called with the *Options/Command prompt* menu item. When this item is activated, you'll be on the OS/2 command line, where you can type commands directly (e.g., DIR). By typing "EXIT", you return to the installation program.

Software configuration menu

Under *Software configuration* you'll find two additional commands for configuring OS/2.

Configuring OS/2 parameters - *Change OS/2 parameters*

By selecting *Software configuration/Change OS/2 parameters*, you can change several OS/2 system parameters. However, these parameters are already optimally set. So, you shouldn't change these settings.

The individual settings have the following meanings:

Printer Monitor Buffer Size

Here, you determine how much data your computer can send to the printer at one time. You can enter quantities between 143 bytes and 2048 bytes. Higher numbers result in a slightly faster printer output.

Buffers

Similar to DOS, OS/2 2.1 also has a buffer. A buffer is a spool of 512 bytes that holds data sent by the hard drive. Having more buffers results in a better data transfer rate from the hard drive. The size suggested is suitable for average hard drives. For very slow hard drives, you should increase the number of buffers (up to a maximum of 100).

Disk cache

This section allows you to set the size, in kilobytes, of your hard drive cache. Similar to a buffer, a disk cache is a spool for data transferred from the hard drive. At this point, you can assign a size from 64K to 7200K. The size of the cache should correspond to the size of the available RAM.

Smaller systems with only 4 Meg of RAM should use 128K to a maximum of 256K of caching. Systems with 8 or more Meg of RAM should use 256K to a maximum of 1024K of caching.

In any case, the optimal size of a cache depends on several factors. To run applications that extensively use the hard drive, you should select a correspondingly larger size for your cache.

Maxwait

The number of seconds entered under *Maxwait* specifies how long before a process is given a higher priority. This means, for example, that a certain keystroke will become more important every 3 seconds.

Swap Minfree

This number determines the size of the swap file. This assigns the minimum storage space, which should be available at all times, to the hard drive. Increase the size of the swap file storage only when there is more space available than you initially indicated.

Threads

This item determines the highest number of threads possible. Threads are operations that are independent of one another. Here you can set the size from 128 to 4095.

Memman Protect

Activating the *Protect* option completely separates the programs from one another, and makes it possible for you to work in Protected mode.

If the *Nonprotect* option is activated, a faulty program, for example, may write into the file area of another program, which is possible under DOS or Windows.

Memman Swap

Activating the *Swap* option helps OS/2 swap programs, which don't need any processing time, into the swap file. Using Swap makes it easy to start many programs. For systems with only 4 or 8 Meg of RAM, leave this option set to *Swap*. For bigger systems with 16 Meg or more, you could activate *Noswap*, at this point, to store all programs in memory.

Priority

This option determines how to divide processing time among the individual programs.

With the default setting, *Dynamic*, the operating system can independently modify the priority of waiting operations according to the specified criteria. With the *Absolute* setting, the system will choose to which operation to assign processing time.

Swappath

With this option you can determine where to place the swap file. This file is usually placed on the boot drive in the directory labeled \OS2\SYSTEM\.

In a computer with two hard drives, you can place the swap file on the second hard drive, for example.

Configuring the DOS parameters - *Change DOS parameters*

Under *Software configuration/Change DOS parameters*, you can modify several DOS system parameters. However, these figures are already optimally set so you shouldn't change them.

The individual settings have the following meanings:

Break

This option has the same meaning as the BREAK=ON/OFF command in DOS. With Break=On active, OS/2 can interrupt a DOS program as soon as OS/2 recognizes a "CTRL-BREAK". If Break=Off is active, the DOS program itself must recognize a "CTRL-BREAK" and react appropriately or it must use a System request operation.

Open FCBS

This allows you to set the number of FCBS (File Control Blocks) that you don't want to close.

If there aren't enough FCBS, the least used FCBS are closed.

Protected FCBS

The number of the protected FCBS must be lower than the maximum number of open FCBS.

RMSIZE

With this setting, you can determine the size, in kilobytes, of the working buffer DOS programs should retain when they are started. Sizes from 256K to 640K are acceptable.

Install push button

Once you've completed all your settings, click on the [Install] button or select *Options/Install* from the menu. The following window is displayed:

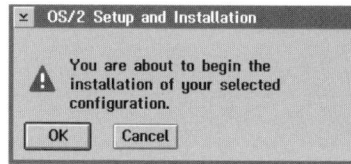

Setup and Installation begins

Once you've inserted the proper diskette, the programs you've selected are copied to your hard disk. After a confirmation message, the installation program will begin copying the remaining diskettes onto the hard drive. A bar chart showing the progress of the installation is displayed for each diskette.

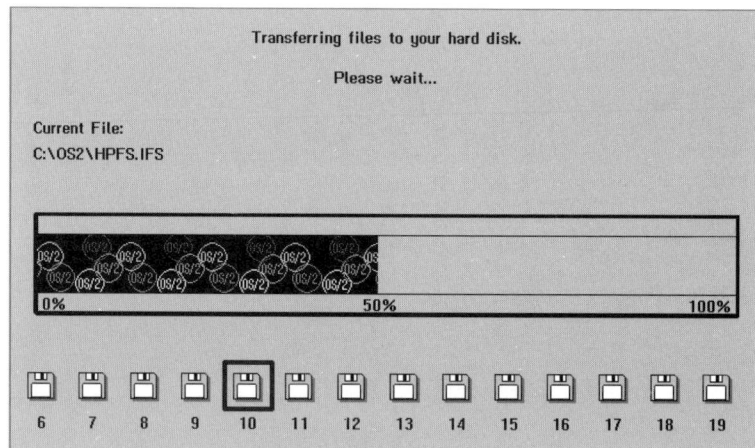

Installation progress

Advanced Options

After you've inserted the entire series of diskettes, you'll see a window for setting the *Advanced Options*.

Install Device Support Diskette

This option will be performed only if you want to install drivers that aren't included within the scope of OS/2. These may include special video drivers and CD-ROM drivers. This was specified when you selected *Other* for a CD-ROM device or a SCSI device. To do this, a "profile control file" must be located on a Device Support Diskette. This file is similar to the OEMSETUP.INF file of Windows.

If the source directory and target directory paths are incorrect, you can enter a new path by using the Change push button.

After the path has been entered correctly, the Installation program searches for the "profile control file" (i.e., the data file), after you've clicked on Install.

You can cancel the installation of the drivers by clicking on Exit.

Migrate Applications

If you have DOS and Windows applications on your hard drive, run this option so that these applications are placed into the OS/2 system environment.

You'll find more information about this option in Section 1.7.

Configure WIN-OS/2 Desktop

Here you can determine how you want to configure the Windows environment under OS/2. You can work with Windows applications in a Windows environment; however, you can run (in VGA mode) Windows applications in a window on the OS/2 Desktop.

Install standard WIN-OS/2 Desktop

With this command, you can install the standard WIN-OS/2 environment. This process doesn't consider any user-specific settings.

Copy WIN-OS/2 Desktop from existing Windows Desktop

This setting enables you to build the WIN-OS/2 environment according to the version of Windows that's already installed on the hard drive.

When you use this setting, you must select *Additional Information* to adjust the path to your existing Windows environment if it's incorrect. If the *Update Windows desktop when WIN-OS/2 desktop is modified* option is activated, any changes made in the

WIN-OS/2 environment will be made automatically by your original Windows.

Preserve WIN-OS/2 desktop currently installed

With this setting, you can accept an already existing WIN-OS/2 environment, if you're installing only a new OS/2.

Click on OK to close the *Configure WIN-OS/2 Desktop* window and activate your selections.

Migrate CONFIG.SYS / AUTOEXEC.BAT

Activate this option if you want to transfer the contents of an existing CONFIG.SYS or AUTOEXEC.BAT to your OS/2 system environment.

This option is available only if you've already installed OS/2 in a partition that's already been formatted (but that hasn't been formatted with HPFS or FAT) and the AUTOEXEC.BAT and CONFIG.SYS files are located in the partition.

Automatically update CONFIG.SYS and AUTOEXEC.BAT

This setting handles all SET, PATH, and DPATH statements. (DPATH is the search path for data, unlike PATH, which is the search path for launching programs.)

User edit CONFIG.SYS and AUTOEXEC.BAT

Activate this option to make any changes yourself. When you click on OK, a window labeled *Edit CONFIG.SYS* appears.

A list of directions appears on the left side of the window. You can insert these directions on the right side.

WARNING

Avoiding Startup Failures

Remember that you're working with the CONFIG.SYS of OS/2. Some changes may cause startup failure in your OS/2 system.

Press F4 to exit this Editor and save the modified CONFIG.SYS file. To exit the Editor without saving the changes, press F5.

Then the AUTOEXEC.BAT window appears. In this window, make changes just as you did in the previous window.

Then you'll return to the *Advanced Options* window. At this point, all the options have been activated. If you want to make additional changes, select the corresponding option.

To continue, click on OK.

The Installation program now begins to update the system configuration of your OS/2 system. This process may take a few minutes. Watch the LED on the hard drive to determine when the process is complete.

1.6   Printer and Display Setup

In a few minutes, the Installation program asks you to insert the first printer driver diskette (Printer Driver Diskette 1) into drive A:. Once you insert the diskette and press Enter, the printer driver previously selected in the System Configuration window is installed.

Display drivers

Next the Installation program asks you to insert the first display driver diskette (Display Driver Diskette 1) into drive A:. Once you insert the diskette and press Enter, the screen displays the drivers selected in the System Configuration window and is installed on your system.

These choices will vary depending on the video driver you selected. These include the following:

- 1024x768x256 colors -1 Meg required

- 640x480x256 colors - 1 Meg or 512K required

- 800x600x256 colors - 1 Meg required

This is usually an automatic process. If you experience any difficulties, contact your graphics card manufacturer.

Installation Complete

Once this is done, the installation of OS/2 is complete. Remove the diskette from the drive and press Enter.

Now OS/2 boots again. During the reboot, OS/2 makes several changes. This is why rebooting this time can take a long time. Later, the time it takes to boot will be noticeably shorter.

WARNING

> **Don't Switch Off Your Computer**
>
> When booting, remember that OS/2 is a complex multitasking system. So, don't switch off the computer at this point because this can cause data loss.
>
> Before you shut down the computer, click the right mouse button on the Desktop to select the *Shutdown* menu item. Then click on OK and switch off the computer when the shutdown process is complete.

DOS Partition

WARNING

> **Note If You Used The Basic Installation and FDISK**
>
> If you used the Basic Installation and used FDISK to partition your hard drive with both an OS/2 HPFS and a DOS FAT file system, you will have to FORMAT the primary DOS partition and install DOS.
>
> To do this, shutdown OS/2 and then restart the computer. Select the DOS partition from the Boot Manager menu. When the computer tries to boot from the hard drive, an error message will be displayed informing you that the hard drive is not formatted.
>
> Insert your DOS installation diskette in drive A: and restart the computer again. Use the DOS installation program to format the hard drive and reinstall DOS. Once DOS is installed you can format any logical partitions so they are accessible from DOS and OS/2.

1.7   Migrate Applications

To use the Windows 3.1 Accessories in OS/2 you must migrate the applications to the OS/2 environment. To make OS/2 migrate DOS and Windows applications into its own environment, open the OS/2 System folder. Then select *System Setup* and *Migrate Applications*, if your hard drive contains any DOS or Windows applications.

In the *Find Programs* window, under the heading *Drives*, you can indicate the drives that should be searched for applications. The system will search all drives that are displayed on a gray background.

OS/2 includes a file (DATABASE.DAT) that contains information on current DOS and Windows applications, as well as information on the necessary settings (DOS settings). You can even expand this file (DATABASE.DAT) by using the PARSEDB program, which is included in OS/2.

In the *Migrate* section you can select the kind of program that should be searched for. This allows you to search for *DOS programs*, *Windows programs*, and *OS/2 programs*. If you don't want to search for a program, click on the check mark to remove it.

Click on [Find] to start the search process.

A window called *Migrate Programs* appears. This window contains a list of all the applications that the Installation program recognizes.

You can exclude some applications by clicking on them once. Only the applications highlighted in gray will be added to the OS/2 desktop.

Click on [Add programs...] if any applications (or programs) aren't listed. An alphabetized list, which contains all the programs that the Installation program has found, appears. Items on this list are sorted according to drive, then to the path, and finally, according to programs.

Use the DOS default settings for any programs you've found in this way. You must adjust these settings later if they need special DOS settings.

Under the heading *Program title*, you can also type any desired title for each program. Later this title will appear as an object or a caption for a window. Under *Parameters*, you can define any parameters you may need and under *Working directory*, you can determine the desired starting directory. Under *Program type*, you must indicate whether each program is a DOS, a Windows, or an OS/2 application.

With the [Add > >] push button, you can insert a program, which was selected in the window, into the group of programs that you want to start under OS/2 later. Any programs you've moved by mistake can be removed with [Remove > >]. You can execute [Add programs] as often as necessary.

When you click [OK], all the programs are transferred to the *Applications* list of programs you want to include in your OS/2 environment.

To transfer all the gray highlighted applications in the *Applications* window, click on the [Migrate] push button. This action transfers the selected applications to the appropriate program groups.

Click on [Exit] to exit the *Migrate Applications* program.

1.8   CONFIG.SYS

For computers with up to 8 Meg of RAM, the installation program provides an ideal configuration. However, you should make the following changes to the configuration file to improve performance. To do this, use the OS/2 System Editor, which is located in the Productivity folder.

More buffers for DOS boxes

To store the DOS kernel in the High Memory Area and to provide DOS with Upper Memory Blocks for TSRs and device drivers, change the line:

```
DOS=LOW,NOUMB
```

to:

```
DOS=HIGH,UMB
```

Increasing cache

A larger disk cache significantly improves performance. For improved performance, change the value given in the first line:

```
IFS=C:\OS2\HPFS.IFS /CACHE:64
```

to:

```
IFS=C:\OS2\HPFS.IFS /CACHE:512
```

Then insert:

```
RUN=C:\OS2\CACHE.EXE /LAZY:ON
```

as the second line.

Adjusting paths

Add the search path for your most important DOS applications to the PATH statement.

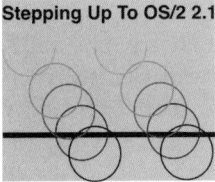

Chapter 2

High Performance File System

The High Performance File System (HPFS) is a new way to manage hard drives. Until now, DOS used a File Allocation Table (FAT). The FAT was developed for CP/M (Control Program for Microprocessors), which is the predecessor of MS-DOS.

When CP/M and its FAT were invented, hard drives didn't exist yet. The FAT was originally intended only for managing diskettes. Therefore, it doesn't operate very efficiently on larger hard drives.

The High Performance File System can manage large hard drives quickly and effectively. Today, a hard disk of 60 Meg or higher is considered large.

Compatibility

The High Performance File System is completely compatible with normal DOS and Windows applications. The application isn't affected regardless of whether it's working with an HPFS or a FAT.

WARNING

> You cannot use any programs that directly access the hard disk, such as a defragmentation utility and the Norton Disk Doctor. These utilities can destroy all data stored on the HPFS hard drive.

Upgrading from DOS 3 to DOS 4, however, caused the same problems. At that time, Microsoft introduced the large partitions and altered their FAT structure. Generally a program that can access a network drive is capable of working with the HPFS.

However, DOS programs cannot use the long filenames and the extended attributes. That's why the long filenames aren't visible under DOS. Also, a file's extended attributes are lost whenever you copy or move files using DOS programs.

Under OS/2, a driver is assigned to each file system. The HPFS driver can work with HPFS disks and FAT disks but the FAT driver cannot read an HPFS disk. So, when you install the High Performance File System, you can easily access all your FAT disks.

> **HINT**
>
> Continue to format diskettes with the familiar FAT format under OS/2. This guarantees trouble-free file swapping with other DOS computers.

2.1   Filenames

The High Performance File System places almost no limits on filenames. The old limitation of an 8 character name and a 3 character extension no longer applies. Under the High Performance File System, filenames can have a maximum of 254 characters.

> **HINT**
>
> Remember that filenames that don't follow the usual FAT rules aren't accessible from the DOS windows and Windows sessions. Most DOS programs would have difficulty operating if the system sent them names that aren't accepted under DOS.

You cannot use certain characters in filenames:

```
"  /  \  :  *  ?  |  <  >  -  &
```

The "@" (at) symbol can be used but it cannot be the first character of a filename.

You can also use periods. Under DOS, periods separate the filenames from their extensions. Since this separation no longer exists with the HPFS, the period is no longer important in filenames.

However, you should continue to use the period to mark certain files. For example, only programs that end with ".EXE" can be launched. Also, text files are still indicated with ".TXT".

The following and similar commands still operate the same way:

```
DIR *.TXT
```

However, there are several exceptions to the file and directory names. The following two names cannot be used in the root directory of a hard drive:

```
PIPE
SEM
```

The following names aren't allowed anywhere because they denote devices in OS/2:

```
KBDS   PRN   NUL
CLOCK$   SCCREEN$   POINTER$   MOUSE$
```

All COMx and LPTx names also cannot be used because these names are address ports. Under the FAT system, all file and directory names appeared in uppercase letters. DOS automatically converts lowercase letters to uppercase letters. The High Performance File System doesn't do this. When you create a directory by typing:

```
MD ThisIsBigAndSmall
```

it will appear exactly like this in the directory. During operation, the system doesn't distinguish between uppercase and lowercase letters.

So you can remove a directory by typing:

```
RD thisisbigandsmall
RD THISISBIGANDSMALL
RD tHISiSbIGaNDsMALL.
```

Long filenames are easier to read if both uppercase and lowercase characters are used. You can also use an underline "_" character or a space.

Type such a name as follows:

```
MD "This Name Is Also Long"
```

Remember to include the quotation marks when spaces are used in a directory or filename.

HINT

> Only a few applications allow spaces or quotation marks in filenames.

To use such a directory or filename as part of a command, you must include the entire path, such as:

```
Copy "This is long\Smith.NIX" A:\
```

The following isn't acceptable because it isn't a valid filename:

```
Copy "This is long"\Smith.NIX A:\
```

2.2   Extended Attributes

The Extended attributes are a new feature of the High
Performance File System. You're probably already familiar with
attributes in DOS. There are four attributes for each file, not
including the date and the time of the last edit.

The HPFS stores additional information about each file. As
before, it retains the time you last edited the file. It also indicates
when you created the file. OS/2 also stores the time and date of
the last access to the file.

HINT

This occurs every time you access the file, even if you
only read it.

To display this information, open drive C:. Now open the *Object*
menu of this drive (right mouse button) and select the
Open/Details View menu item. A chart, displaying all the
information, appears:

Icon	Title	Real name	Size	Last write date	Last write time	Last access date	Last a
	OS/2 2.0 Desktop	OSI2 21.0 Desktop	0	2-8-93	2:42:18 PM	2-8-93	
	OS/2 2.0 Desktop	OSI2 2.0 Desktop	0	2-8-93	2:36:24 PM	2-8-93	
	Nowhere	Nowhere	0	2-8-93	2:36:26 PM	2-8-93	
	OS2	OS2	0	2-8-93	12:19:40 PM	2-8-93	
	PSFONTS	PSFONTS	0	2-8-93	12:31:22 PM	2-8-93	
	SPOOL	SPOOL	0	2-8-93	2:35:54 PM	2-8-93	
	ACLLOCK.LST	ACLLOCK.LST	71	2-9-93	1:39:22 PM	2-9-93	
	AUTOEXEC.BAK	AUTOEXEC.BAK	264	2-8-93	2:19:54 PM	2-9-93	
	AUTOEXEC.BAT	AUTOEXEC.BAT	263	2-9-93	2:30:26 PM	2-9-93	
	CONFIG.BAK	CONFIG.BAK	2,118	2-9-93	11:54:54 AM	2-9-93	
	CONFIG.SYS	CONFIG.SYS	2,147	2-9-93	2:46:26 PM	2-9-93	
	OS2DUMP	OS2DUMP	3,096	12-9-92	3:41:10 PM	2-9-93	
	OS2LDR.MSG	OS2LDR.MSG	8,447	12-9-92	3:41:00 PM	2-9-93	
	README	README	18,711	12-15-92	1:40:54 PM	2-9-93	

Details View of drive C:

This window is divided into two sections that display information
about the file. The arrows at the bottom of the window are used to
scroll the display.

Under *Size*, the size of the file is indicated in bytes.

The *Last write date* and *Last write time* columns indicate the last
time the file was written to (i.e., edited). *Creation date* and
Creation time indicate the date the file was created.

Last access date and *Last access time* display the time the file was last accessed. This includes accessing the file only to read it.

The system attributes are located under *Flags*:

File Attributes	
R	Read Only
A	Archive
H	Hidden
S	System

These are identical to the normal DOS attributes.

So far this information is similar to the information provided under DOS. Now we'll discuss the Extended attributes.

Real Name	is the regular filename that you see when you type DIR to display the contents of a directory.
Title	is the name that the Workplace Shell displays. At the same time, the Workplace Shell displays an *Icon*. The *Icon* and *Title* are parts of the Workplace Shell.

While the file system continues to work with the *Real Name*, the Workplace Shell, on the other hand, uses a different filename or *Title*.

This process allows the Workplace Shell to work with long filenames even on a FAT disk. At the same time, it can manage several different similarly named files in one folder.

Windows does something similar in its program groups. In a Windows program group you enter both the real filename and the program title.

The Workplace Shell name is stored in the extended attributes, which store information about a file.

Windows also contains data for and about a file. For example, for DOS programs, Windows uses PIF files. These files are located in the directory as individual files. When you copy or move programs, you must remember these PIF files. OS/2 2.1 stores the information in the PIF file in the directory entry.

The directory entry of each file contains certain information:

- Where the file is located on the hard drive

- The size of the file

- The file attributes (RAHS)

- The various clock times and dates

- The name of the file

Under OS/2 2.1, the data stored here is expandable. Because this data is now an integral part of the directory structure; the operating system will automatically address them at every file operation.

OS/2 2.1 stores extended attributes in a hidden file in the root directory of the corresponding drive whenever it works with a FAT disk. This is called the "EA DATA.SF" file. The system immediately opens this file so its data is available. It also does this for diskettes.

The Workplace Shell writes its own filenames and the icon in these extended attributes.

HINT

> You cannot access the extended attributes from the command line. REXX, the new batch programming language of OS/2 2.1, contains functions for working with extended attributes.

The LAN manager stores passwords and access authorizations for each file in these extended attributes.

2.3   Caching

The High Performance File System works with a built-in disk cache. This means that you don't need any external programs or drivers, such as Hyperdisk or SmartDrive.

Set the size of the cache in the CONFIG.SYS:

```
IFS=C:\OS2\HPFS.IFS   /CACHE:1024 /CRECL:4 /AUTOCHECK:CD
```

The statement "/CACHE:xxxx" is indicated in kilobytes. The maximum allowed is 2 Meg.

Include all HPFS drives under Autocheck, if possible. Autocheck automatically checks the system structures of the drives. If there aren't any problems, this check is performed quickly.

Don't modify the CRECL statement if possible. It's used to access the cache's internal manager.

In relation to FAT, Lazy Write is also a new feature. If you've worked with Hyperdisk under DOS, you should be familiar with this procedure as Staggered Write. This refers to a type of shifted writing. By executing not only read accesses, but also write accesses in buffers, Lazy Write significantly improves performance.

```
RUN=C:\OS2\CACHE.EXE /LAZY:ON /MAXAGE:20000 /DISKIDLE:5000
        /BUFFERIDLE:2000
```

CACHE.EXE has four options:

Lazy	allows direct write optimization. This can be set to ON or OFF.
Maxage	sets the latest time limit for writing data to the hard drive. This setting is indicated in milliseconds. Since the write buffer is emptied only when the hard drive isn't busy, write accesses are shifted to times when the hard drive isn't being used.
DiskIdle	sets the time, in milliseconds, during which the drive shouldn't be working.

After a certain interval has passed, when reading or writing to the disk hasn't occurred, the cache assumes that something is wrong and writes all the buffers to the hard drive.

BufferIdle	sets the amount of time the computer should remain idle.

Entering CACHE at the OS/2 command line will display the current settings. The example previously given includes settings that are slightly higher than the default settings. Although this increases speed, these settings use more buffers and are slightly more dangerous.

WARNING

> **You Must Use The Desktop's Shutdown Feature**
>
> When the cache is optimizing the write function, you must use the Desktop's Shutdown feature. Simply switching off the computer can cause data loss. To further improve the system's performance, you can increase BUFFERS=20 in the CONFIG.SYS. Each buffer occupies 512 bytes.

The Swap file feature of OS/2 2.1 isn't cached.

A cache created under DISKCACHE=512.LW,AC:E in the CONFIG.SYS doesn't affect the HPFS. Only a FAT disk is affected.

2.4   How HPFS Operates

The HPFS uses a different kind of organization than the FAT system. In this section, we'll briefly discuss this organization.

HPFS original design

The HPFS was originally designed for the LAN manager. This is a network server like the widely used Novell Netware. However, you can install SQL servers or other servers on the LAN manager.

When working with database servers, huge files can accumulate quickly. Because of this, these computers must have larger disks.

The HPFS is designed for these types of computers. So it's capable of dealing with large drives and large files. To fully use the capabilities of the High Performance File System, avoid dividing your hard drive into many tiny partitions, which DOS users generally do.

Several small partitions interfere with HPFS's many advantages. Also, you shouldn't be afraid to install huge files; the HPFS can easily work with these files.

Saving space

In the FAT system, all sectors are numbered sequentially. This wasn't a problem as long as there were only a few sectors. Since the FAT system uses 16 bit numbers for this numbering, the number of sectors couldn't exceed 65,534. For a sector size larger than 512 bytes, this meant that a hard drive couldn't be larger than 32 Meg.

There are two ways you can use the FAT system on large hard drives. Either use more bits per number or increase the size of the sectors. Since the first method would cause compatibility problems, the developers chose the second method.

Imagine a step between FAT numbering and sector numbering. The result is a cluster. A cluster consists of a group of sequential sectors. The amount of sectors you can group in a cluster depends on the size of the disk. A small cluster can contain 4 sectors and the largest cluster can contain 64 sectors.

Unfortunately, a lot of space is wasted on the disk. Each file occupies entire clusters. However, it's unlikely that the file will fill up its clusters completely. So there are always a few kilobytes that are not in use even though they are partially occupied.

So, theoretically a 1 byte file could occupy a 32K cluster. This obviously wastes a lot of disk space. Even on medium-sized hard drives, the wasted space can amount to several megabytes.

The High Performance File System returns to direct sector access. Clusters aren't used in this system. As a result, the system eliminates this waste of disk space.

Speed

When compared to the FAT system, the High Performance File System works much faster.

In a FAT file system, the File Allocation Table and the directory are always located on the disk first. So, in the extreme case, this means that at each file access the read-write head must travel once across the entire hard drive.

In the HPFS, the directory is located midway around the disk, so that even in the worst case, the head must travel only half the disk. This simple trick decreases the access time by half.

In the FAT, all the directory items aren't listed in any order. HPFS sorts these items alphabetically on a B tree. While the FAT must search the entire tree for an item, HPFS can directly access any file on its tree.

The HPFS was designed to use a disk cache. Since this capability is firmly integrated in the logic of the system, it works very efficiently. However, the DOS cache programs weren't designed to be used with the FAT, so some disk problems can occur.

Another improvement is the division of volumes into tracks. In the FAT system, a file management area is located first; the data area is located behind it.

In the HPFS system, 8 Meg of data is always accompanied by its corresponding management area. The data and their management area are located next to each other. This decreases the amount the read/write head must be moved to access a file.

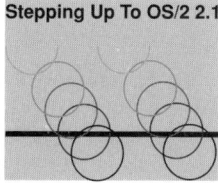

Chapter 3

—— Workplace Shell ——

The Workplace Shell (WPS) is the new interface of OS/2 2.1. It replaces the Presentation Manager (PM). The PM, which was the model for Windows 3 interface, was the result of an IBM SAA (System Application Architecture) project.

The SAA project describes all possible interfaces for programs. It's supposed to simplify program usage on different computers by standardizing these interfaces. For the user, standardized interfaces are helpful because all the programs look and work the same way. This part of the SAA project is called CUA, Common User Access.

The first description of CUA, called CUA89, was published in 1989. Windows 3 is based on this description. Even the SAA interface, which is widely distributed as part of DOS, is based on CUA89.

The latest Workplace Shell is based on CUA91. Although the CUA89 is still considered one of the classical interfaces, CUA91 represents the interface of the future.

The Workplace Shell works as an object-oriented environment. However, it's easy to adapt to the new Workplace Shell.

The first CUA91 programs have already appeared under Windows 3, which is a sign that CUA91 is a major advancement in interfaces. For example, the new Quattro Pro for Windows, by Borland, works exactly like the Workplace Shell. Many publishers have announced OS/2 2.1 versions of their programs.

The Workplace Shell's design is based on a completely different philosophy than that of the old CUA89 interfaces. However, a smooth conversion is possible with the Workplace Shell. You can continue to work almost as you always have but you can gradually discover the new capabilities and learn how to use them.

We won't demonstrate how to use the windows of the Workplace Shell, the OS/2 tutorial does an excellent job. Most likely you already know how to close and move windows. These operations are performed by using the Title-bar icon and the title bar.

The Maximize and Minimize buttons are also the same. To change the size of a window, click on its frame and move the mouse. Also, you can activate programs by double-clicking. Directories and program groups are also opened the same way.

3.1   Startup Screen

The OS/2 startup screen may look familiar if you've worked with an Atari ST, Macintosh, or GEM operating system. A Shredder icon appears in the lower-right corner. A Printer icon appears in the upper-left corner.

The drive icons are displayed in the lower-right portion of the screen. Your screen may differ slightly, depending on your installation of OS/2 and if you are attached to a network.

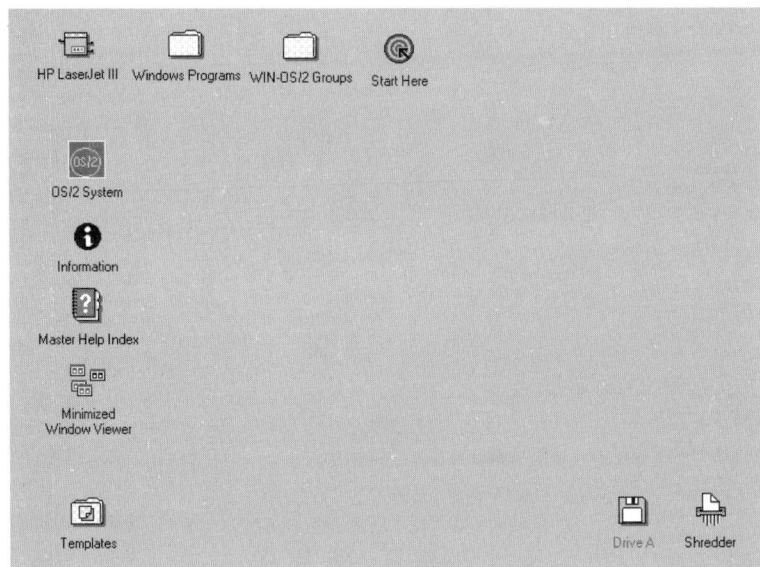

Workplace Shell startup screen

The *OS/2 System* icon is a program group that contains the *System Setup* program, the *Productivity* folder, the *Games* folder, the *Startup* folder, the *Drives* icon, and the *Command Prompts* folder.

As we mentioned, your startup screen may look slightly different. During the first startup, the icons aren't arranged in any particular order.

In fact, all the icons may not even appear on your screen. For example, only the Drive A: icon may appear on the desktop.

Before you can organize your personal Workplace Shell and since the Workplace Shell is an object-oriented environment, we must first explain the concept of "objects".

3.2   Object Menu

Everything you see on the screen is an object: the icons, the printer, the program groups, and even the desktop are objects. Each object has certain characteristics and capabilities. For example, the printer can print files, a diskette can be formatted, and a program can display information in a window.

Objects are always grouped in a folder; even the desktop itself is a folder. The Desktop menu is a normal folder object menu.

Every object has its own menu. This Object menu contains all the possible operations that you can execute with the object. Once a window is open, you can activate the Object menu in exactly the same way as the Control menu in Windows.

Click on the box next to the window title. The Object menu and the Control menu are identical in OS/2 2.1. You can also simply click the right mouse button on an empty area inside the open window to open the Object menu.

When the window is closed and only its icon is visible, click the right mouse button on its icon to open the Object menu.

A small menu appears:

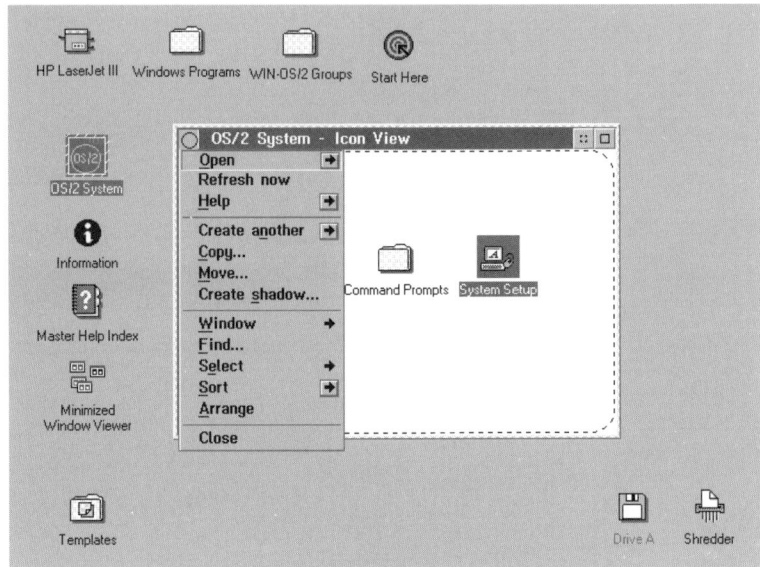

Object menu

HINT

Unlike Windows, OS/2 2.1 uses both mouse buttons. You can assign any setting to these buttons in the *System Setup* program.

In this window, you can select the menu items under Window either by clicking on it or by using the cursor keys and Enter.

When an arrow appears next to a menu choice, that choice contains a submenu. You can open a submenu by clicking on the arrow.

HINT

Only active choices are displayed in object menus.

Object menus have a set number of choices. Although these choices appear in every object menu, they are rarely used. Instead, a shortcut procedure or key combination is used. This is similar to closing a window in Windows.

For example, you can open the Control menu and select *Close* to close an open window. However, usually you'll simply double-click on the Title-bar icon in the left corner of the title bar to close the window.

3.3   Setting Up the Workplace Shell

When setting up the Workplace Shell, first you must clean up the desktop so you can organize the objects. Since the Workplace Shell is so flexible, it's possible to create a completely different kind of workplace.

First, find and select the *Shredder* icon. This is OS/2 2.1's trash can.

Shredder

The Shredder

HINT

> This icon looks like a document shredder. However, don't confuse this icon with the printer icon, which looks similar.

Place the mouse pointer over the *Shredder*. Now hold down the right mouse button. Move the mouse back and forth across the screen. The *Shredder* should move along with your mouse pointer on the screen. Now move the mouse to the lower-right corner of the screen. Release the mouse button again and the *Shredder* remains in place. You've just moved the first object across your desktop.

HINT

> If scroll bars appear when you do this, you've moved the *Shredder* too close to the edge. When objects are moved off the desktop, scroll bars appear. This occurs because all the objects cannot fit into one window. To solve this problem, select the *Shredder* and drag it towards the center of the screen.

While you were dragging the *Shredder* across the desktop, you may have noticed that its appearance changed several times. Each time you drag one object over another, either a frame or a veto symbol (⊘) appears. The frame indicates that you can place the Shredder over this object. A veto (⊘) symbol indicates that you cannot place the *Shredder* over this object. Try the following:

HINT

> Carefully move the *Shredder* over other icons. If you place an icon on the *Shredder*, OS/2 2.1 thinks you want to throw it away and deletes it. Although in this case, you're placing the *Shredder* on another icon, you should still be careful.

Locate the *Printer* icon and place it in the upper-left corner of the screen. To do this, place the mouse on the icon and hold down the right mouse button. Now move the icon to the corner and release the mouse button.

NEC CP7+

The Printer icon

Move the *OS/2 System*, *Information*, and *Master Help Index* icons to the left side of the screen. The program groups should be located at the side of the screen.

Now you should have an organized, clutter-free screen. The *Drive A* icon already appears on the desktop in the lower-right corner. However, the other drives are missing; at the very least, the C drive is missing. Also missing will be a second disk drive or other hard drives if they are part of your computer system.

Open the *OS/2 System* program group by double-clicking it. You will find other program groups here. Since the objects we're looking for are in the *Drives* group, open this group now.

WARNING

> This takes a few seconds because OS/2 first checks to see which drives you have. Then it creates the drive objects.

What happens next will be new for Windows users but familiar to GEM users. A rubber band is dragged with the mouse to select multiple objects. This rubber band is used to select objects. All objects inside the rubber band are selected. The selected objects are displayed with a colored background. Under Windows, you select several objects by holding down (Shift) and clicking all the desired icons.

To pull a rubber band, simply move the mouse while holding down the left mouse button. The computer then draws a rectangle that is defined by two points. The first point is the mouse position where you began pressing the left mouse button and the second point is the current mouse position.

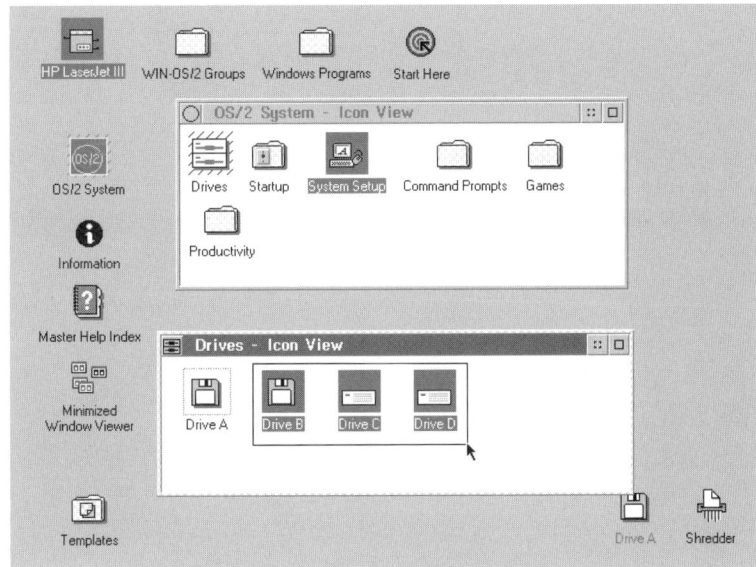

The rubber band

If you've selected several objects, you can manage them like a single selected object. For example, all the objects can be dragged to the *Shredder*.

If you open the Object menu of one of the selected objects, the operation applies to all the selected files. For example, if you select *Copy*, then all the files will be copied.

WARNING

> Each window has its own set of selected files. This means that if you select objects in two different windows and perform an operation, only the current window is affected.

Since a rubber band is always shaped like a rectangle, you can use it to select only icons that are next to each other. To select other icons, you must use the Ctrl key. Hold down Ctrl and select the desired icons with the left mouse button.

Now use a rubber band to select the drives that are missing from the Desktop. In our example, these are drives B to D. Move the drives to the Desktop. Hold down the right mouse button and move the mouse pointer with the icons to the Desktop outside the window.

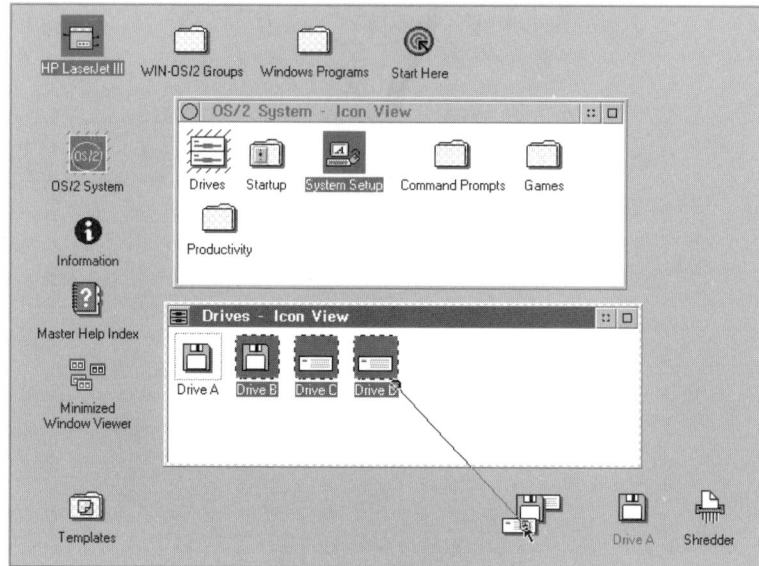

A Shadow appears

As you're doing this, notice a line running from the original icon in the window to your mouse. This line disappears when you release the right mouse button to drop the drives onto the Workplace Shell desktop.

WARNING

A Note On Moving Objects

Some objects cannot be moved from their original window. A shadow is created when you try to move these objects. This shadow represents the original object. The system considers the drives in this window as templates. We'll discuss templates in more detail later in this chapter.

Now sort the drives starting with drive A:, which is already in the window. When this is done, you're ready to use the Desktop.

HINT

You must shut down the system to save the positions of the icons. This is similar to quitting the Program Manager in Windows. However, shutting down the system in OS/2 2.1 is more important than in Windows. This is especially true if you're working with the High Performance File System.

To do shut down, close all the windows. An empty Desktop with a row of icons appears on the screen. Place the mouse in the middle of the Desktop; make certain no icons are below the mouse. Click the right mouse button. The Object menu of the Workplace Shell desktop appears:

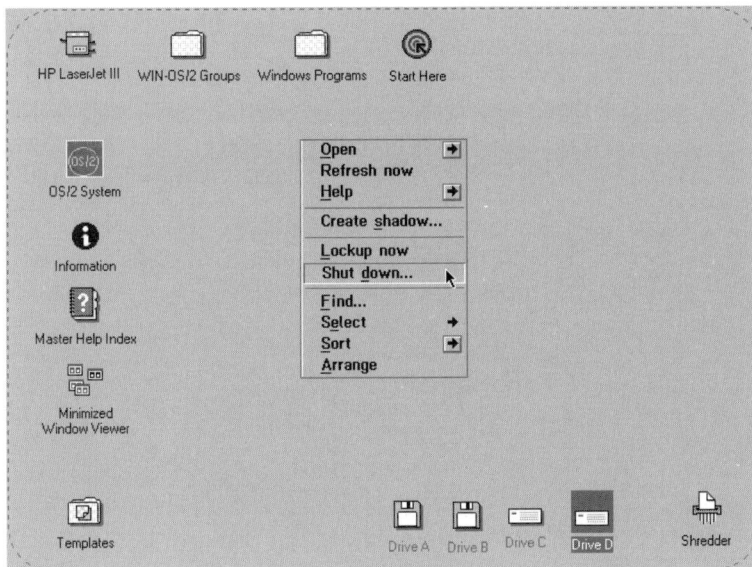

Desktop menu

This menu contains an item called *Shut down*. Select this menu item by clicking it. The screen clears and a security prompt appears, asking whether you really want to shut down. Answer the prompt with ⌷OK⌷. After a while, a message appears informing you that you can switch off the computer or reboot.

Now press ⌷Ctrl⌷+⌷Alt⌷+⌷Del⌷ to restart your computer. The Workplace Shell desktop should appear on the screen again after the booting process is finished.

3.4   Working with Objects

In this section we'll discuss all the operations you can perform with objects. However, since many objects are discussed in their own section, we won't repeat the information here. Also we'll discuss creating a new object in the section on templates.

Opening an object

You can open (start) programs by double-clicking the appropriate icon. If you double-click the *Printer* icon, the *Print Job List* appears. The Print Manager under Windows operates the same way. You can also open folders by double-clicking them. The *Shredder* is the only object you cannot open.

Instead of double-clicking, you could also select *Open* from the Object menu. Then select the appropriate submenu item, such as *Program* to start a program.

If you try to start a data file, the matching application is automatically loaded with the file. Windows also has this capability, but it functions differently.

Selecting objects

You can use either the rubber band, the mouse or the Object menu to select objects.

Rubber band

Use the mouse to stretch the rubber band. All the objects inside the rubber band are selected and displayed on a colored background.

WARNING

> To deselect the files, click the left mouse button on an empty area in the window.

Object menu

Certain Object menus contain the *Select* item. You can choose either *Select all*, which selects all the files in the corresponding window, or *Deselect all*, which cancels all the selections.

Copying and moving objects

To move an object from one window to another, simply move the icon to the new window. First position the mouse over the object you want to move. Then hold down the right mouse button. The object sticks to your mouse pointer and you can move it through the area. Move the mouse to the desired window and release the mouse button. The object remains in the new location.

To display the object in both windows, you must copy it. Copying a file is similar to moving a file, except that you must hold down the Ctrl key as you move the mouse pointer. You could also use the Object menu to do this. Select the files and open the Object menu of one of the selected objects.

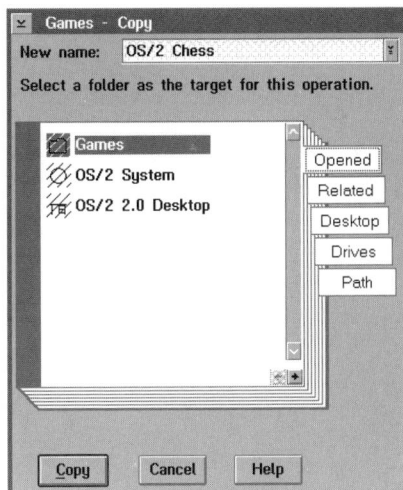

Copy Notebook

A notebook appears on the screen. OS/2 uses this notebook for many procedures. You can scroll through the different pages by selecting the tabbed dividers. The *Opened* page contains all the windows that are currently open. You can select one of these windows and select Copy to begin copying.

Related contains all the directories on the same level and below the current search directory. *Desktop* contains all the folders that are on the Desktop. The opened folders appear in a shaded background.

Under *Drives* you will find all the drives known to your system. However, you always copy files in the root directory. So this window is only useful for floppy diskettes.

Under *New Name* you can specify a new filename, which applies to all copied files. OS/2 2.1 is able to manage several files of the same name in one directory. We'll see exactly how this works in the drive windows.

Under *Path* you can enter a target path.

Deleting objects

To delete an object, simply drag it to the *Shredder*. You could also use *Delete* from the Object menu. Then you'll be asked whether you really want to delete the files.

To delete entire subdirectories, disable the *Confirm on folder delete* check box. Also, disable the *Confirm on delete* check box if you don't want to confirm each delete process.

WARNING

> You can disable both of these check boxes for the entire system in *System Settings* in the *OS/2 System* folder.

OS/2 2.1 provides an undelete function. However, this function is integrated in the file system instead of the Workplace Shell. To recover a file, open a command shell.

Shells are located in the *OS/2 System* folder under *Command Prompts*. Start the OS/2 Shell. It doesn't matter whether you use *OS/2 Full screen* or *OS/2 Window*. Then change to the directory containing the deleted files.

Enter UNDELETE to begin recovering the files. This is similar to the DOS UNDELETE command.

To delete a shadow with its original, open the *Original* submenu in the Object menu. Then select *Delete*. This deletes the current shadow, its original, and any other shadows. If you delete only the shadow, the original object isn't affected. We'll explain shadows later in this chapter.

Printing objects

To print a file, drag it to the printer. The file is then placed in the printer spooler and printed. You could also select *Print* from the Object menu. If you installed more than one printer, a submenu appears under *Print*. This submenu displays a list of printers, from which you can select the one you want to use.

However, the easiest method to print the document is directly from the application. Most programs now provide print preview and similar help functions. However, the Workplace Shell desktop doesn't have these functions.

You can view a print job in the spooler. Open the spooler window by double-clicking the printer object. Then double-click the print job. The *Picture Viewer* appears with the printout.

Shadow objects

In OS/2 2.1, a file can have a shadow. This means there can be different directory entries that point to the same file. So a file can appear in several directories but occupy space on the hard drive only once.

WARNING

> **Shadows Exist Only Within The Workplace Shell**
>
> Unlike Unix, the High Performance File System doesn't allow file links. The Workplace Shell saves these shadows in the extended attributes of the directory entry.

These shadows are used to make program groups under OS/2 2.1. The principle used here should be familiar to Unix users. You use a directory as a program group and then place shadows of all the programs in this directory. When you display this directory, all the programs seem to be in the directory.

You can create one or more shadows for each object. This means that you can also have multiple shadows of folders, printers, or drives.

If you delete a shadow, the original object isn't affected. This also occurs in Windows. If you delete a program in a Program group, it isn't physically deleted from the hard drive. Instead, only its entry is removed from the Program group.

WARNING

> If you delete an object, all of its shadows also disappear.

Creating a shadow is similar to copying or moving a file, except that you hold down Ctrl+Shift and move the object to the target window. While you're moving the object, a line appears between the original object and the new shadow.

You can also create a shadow by using *Create Shadow* from the Object menu. Use different options to determine the destination.

All currently opened windows are displayed on the *Opened* page. Select one of these windows and use Create to begin the process. *Desktop* contains all the folders that are on the Desktop. The opened folders are shaded.

Under *Drives* you'll find all the drives known to your system. Since files are always loaded in the root directory, this window is only practical for diskettes. Enter a target path under *Path*.

Select Create to make shadows of the files.

WARNING

Since shadows behave exactly like the originals, at first you won't be able to tell them apart. To distinguish between the shadows and the original, open the Object menu. If *Original* is one of the choices, you're working with a shadow.

A submenu with three choices is available under *Original*. If you select *Locate*, the Workplace Shell places the window on the screen along with the original. If you select *Copy*, the original also appears on the screen, but is immediately selected. This also starts the normal copying process. To delete the original, select *Original/Delete*. This deletes the original and all of its reflections.

Renaming objects

To rename an object, hold down [Alt] and click on the object name. The name, which is located directly under the icon, changes into an entry line, on which you can enter the new name. Use the [Enter] key to start a new line, this new line won't be displayed until you finish editing the name. When you're finished, click your mouse in an empty area near the icon or on the icon itself.

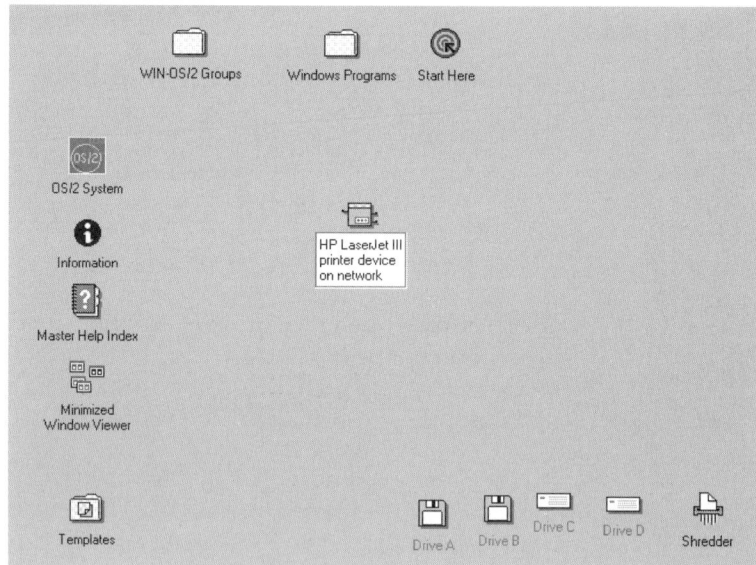

Renaming the printer object

You can also use the Object menu to do this. Simply enter the new name on the *General* page under *Title*.

3.5   Drive Windows

If you installed the Workplace Shell according to our recommendations, then all the drives are on the Desktop. Otherwise, they are in the *Drives* folder in the *OS/2 System* program group. You can either work with them there or copy them to the Desktop.

HINT

> The root directory of the OS/2 boot drive contains the Desktop directory. This directory, along with all of its subdirectories, manages the Workplace Shell of your Desktop. So you shouldn't change this directory. You can also perform all operations with the Workplace Shell.

Opening drive windows

Let's open the window for the boot drive. Select the boot drive Object menu and then select *Open/Tree View*. You'll notice that this window is similar to the File Manager of Windows. This window displays a directory tree.

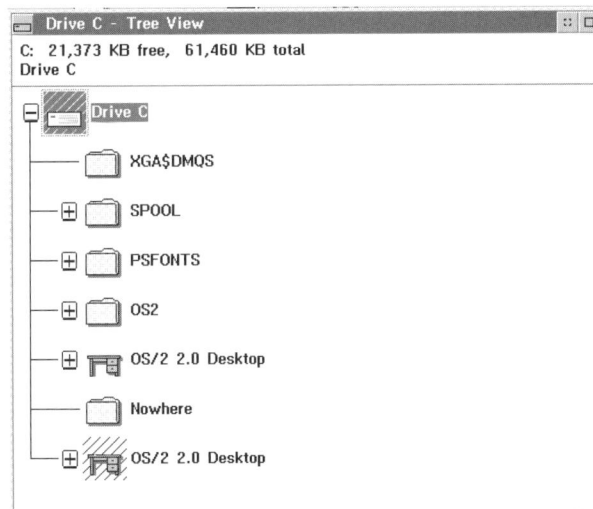

```
Drive C - Tree View                              :: □
C: 21,373 KB free,  61,460 KB total
Drive C

  Drive C

        XGA$DMQS

    +   SPOOL

    +   PSFONTS

    +   OS2

    +   OS/2 2.0 Desktop

        Nowhere

    +   OS/2 2.0 Desktop
```

Drive window

Information about the available disk space and total size of the hard drive is displayed at the top of the window.

You can open and close the tree by using the addition (+) and subtraction (-) signs in front of the directory names. This functions just like the File Manager of Windows.

Now double-click one of the directory icons to open *Icon View*. This corresponds to the right window of the File Manager. However, unlike the File Manager, the Workplace Shell also displays the program icons.

WARNING

> The Workplace Shell uses the regular OS/2 and Windows icons for their programs. Since DOS programs don't have their own icons, the Workplace Shell uses default icons. This also applies to directories and data objects.

You can move, copy, delete, and open objects here, just as we described earlier.

Details View works the same way. To activate *Details View*, select *Open/Details View* in the Object menu of the drive window. All the information about the files is located there.

Searching for files

There are two ways to find files. You can use *Seek and Scan Files*, which is in the *Productivity* folder. This is definitely the most efficient way to find files. However, you can also use the *Find* window, which is accessed from the Object menu of an open drive window. When you select *Find*, a window appears on the screen.

After *Name* type the name of the file you want to find. You can use the wildcards * and ?. For example, type "*.PAS" to find all the Pascal files on your hard drive. Usually a single star appears next to *Name*. This indicates that all the files will be found.

In the *Type* field, specify the type of file to be found. This is an additional filter.

Use the check boxes *Search just this folder* and *Search all Subfolders* to determine where the search should take place. *Search just this folder* searches only the current directory and *Search all Subfolders* searches the current directory and all of its subdirectories.

To search the entire hard drive, go to the root directory and activate *Search all Subfolders*.

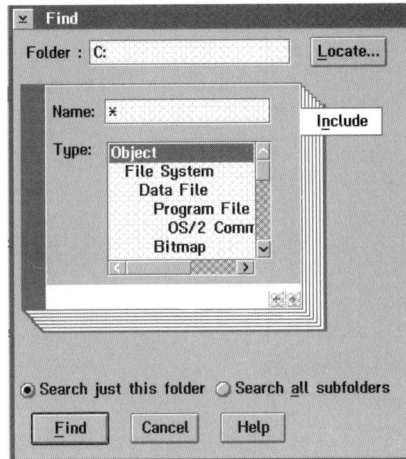

Find window

The search directory is displayed in *Folder*. Select *Locate* to display a window in which you can set the directory.

The results of the search are then displayed in a newly created program group. This program group is called *Find Result* and is followed by the search mask.

You can work with the icons using this program group. However, once you're finished, you can delete the program group again.

Formatting diskettes

To format a diskette, open the Object menu of the appropriate drive icon and select *Format Disk* .... A new window appears on the screen.

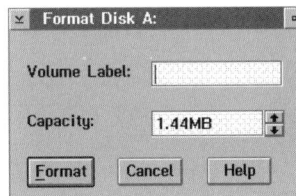

Floppy Disk window

Enter the name of the diskette under *Volume Label*. You can change this name later if necessary.

Use *Capacity* to define the format of the diskette. Only the proper format will be provided. For example, you cannot format a 5.25" diskette at 1.44 megabytes.

If you format a hard drive, the prompt for the capacity doesn't apply. However, you are able to choose between formatting the drive with the High Performance File System or the FAT system.

```
┌─────────────────────────────────────────┐
│ ⌄  Format Disk D:                      □ │
├─────────────────────────────────────────┤
│                                          │
│   Volume Label:   │DOS & OS/2│           │
│                                          │
│   ┌─File System Type─────────────────┐   │
│   │ ○ HPFS (High Performance File System) │
│   │ ◉ FAT (File Allocation Table)    │   │
│   └──────────────────────────────────┘   │
│                                          │
│   ┌──────┐  ┌──────┐  ┌──────┐          │
│   │Format│  │Cancel│  │ Help │          │
│   └──────┘  └──────┘  └──────┘          │
└─────────────────────────────────────────┘
```

Hard Disk Format Disk window

WARNING

> Since OS/2 2.1 is a true multitasking system, you can format diskettes in the background without any problems. So this process won't slow down your work in other programs.

A window, displaying the progress in percentages, appears. When the bar reaches 100%, the OK button is released and you can click it to close this window.

Checking diskettes

The Workplace Shell allows you to execute the CHKDSK command from the Desktop. This command is used to check for defective diskettes. For example, a diskette can become defective when it's removed from the disk drive during a write procedure.

To check a diskette, open the Object menu of the appropriate drive icon. Then select *Check Disk....* In the window that appears, activate the *Write corrections to disk* check box to correct the errors.

WARNING

> You can activate this check box only if the hard drive isn't being used. If files are still open on the hard drive, an error message is displayed. This is also why you cannot use this command to repair drive C:. However, you don't need to use this command for drive C: because this drive is automatically checked for errors when you boot the system.

Click the Check button to start the process. The file system is displayed at the top of the window that appears. The system can be FAT or HPFS. The total capacity and free disk space are also displayed in this window.

A pie representing total capacity is displayed under *Current Usage*. The individual slices of the pie are displayed in different colors.

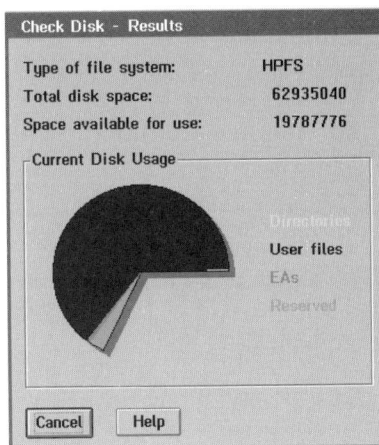

The status of the diskette

The pie is divided into four parts. Normal files (i.e., programs and their data) are in *User Files*. *EA* refers to the space on your hard drive occupied by Extended Attributes. This part is usually quite small. The same applies to *Reserved* and *Directories*. The file management data are in *Reserved*. The space occupied by directory structures appears under *Directories*.

To close the window, select Cancel.

Changing the sorting sequence

You can sort files according to name or type. Both of these options are available in the Object menu under the *Sort* menu item. The setting applies to the current window and all the windows that can be opened from here by double-clicking an icon.

WARNING

This setting is only temporary. It is lost as soon as you close the window.

To change the sorting sequence permanently, open the drive window. Then activate *Open/Settings* in the Object menu. On the *Sort* page, set the *Object Type* to *Object* and set *Default sort attribute* to *Name* or *Type*. Then enable *Always maintain sort order* and close the notebook.

Arranging icons

When you resize a window, you can change the arrangement of the icons with the *Arrange* menu item in the Object menu of the window.

Free disk space

To determine how much disk space is still free on a hard drive or a diskette, open the Object menu of the drive icon. Under *Open/Settings*, the *Details* page lists all the important information about the drive.

Changing partitions

You can also call the FDISK command from the Workplace Shell desktop. There are two versions of FDISK: the text version and the graphic version. You may have already seen the text-oriented command during installation.

Once you're in the command line, activate the text version of FDISK with:

```
FDISK
```

The graphic version is called:

```
FDISKPM
```

and switches back to the Workplace Shell. To call this version directly from the Workplace Shell, open the OS/2 System group. The Object menu of the Drives icon contains the *Create Partition* item.

```
┌─────────────────────────────────────────────────────────┬─────┐
│ ▣  Fixed Disk Utility                                    │ □ □ │
│ Options   Help                                                  │
├─────────────────────────────────────────────────────────┴─────┤
│ ┌──────────┐                                                    │
│ │ ▭      1 │                                                    │
│ └──────────┘                                                    │
│                                                                 │
│ Partition Information                                           │
│                                                                 │
│ Name          Status          Access      File System Type  MBytes │
│ ┌───────────────────────────────────────────────────────────┐ │
│ │ DOS 6.0      Bootable        :Primary     FAT              17│▲│
│ │              None          D :Logical     FAT              40│ │
│ │ OS/2 2.1     Bootable      C :Primary     HPFS             60│ │
│ │              Startable       :Primary     BOOT MANAGER      1│ │
│ │                                                            │ │
│ │                                                            │ │
│ │                                                            │▼│
│ └───────────────────────────────────────────────────────────┘ │
└─────────────────────────────────────────────────────────────────┘
```

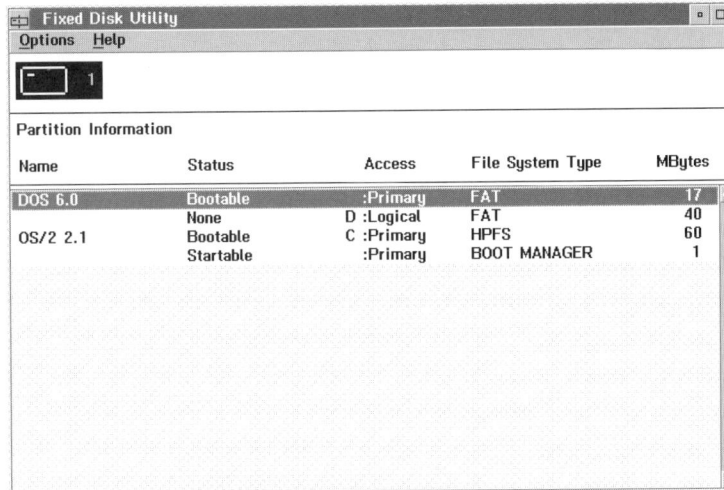

The FDISKPM, Fixed Disk Utility Program

HINT

> Before starting this program, quit all your applications. If you make changes to the partition table you must reboot the computer.

Once you're familiar with the text version, you should also be able to use the graphic version.

3.6 Program Groups Are No Longer Necessary

Program groups in Windows are separate files, in which the programs that belong to the corresponding group, are managed. Icons and paths are stored in these files.

OS/2 2.1 doesn't actually have program groups. The Workplace Shell has something that performs the same tasks, but works differently.

As you read earlier, the Desktop is simply a directory. For example, open the drive window of your boot drive. A directory called Desktop is located in this window. Now open the tree beneath this directory by clicking on the addition sign in front of it. This displays additional directories. These directories match the folders on the Desktop.

At the very least, you should see OS/2 System and one or two program groups here. If you've organized the Workplace Shell according to our suggestions, the Desktop directory should also appear.

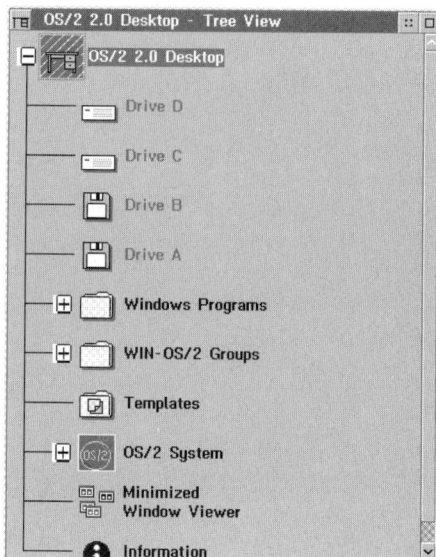

OS/2 2.0 Desktop - Tree View

OS/2 2.0 Desktop

Drive D

Drive C

Drive B

Drive A

Windows Programs

WIN-OS/2 Groups

Templates

OS/2 System

Minimized Window Viewer

Information

OS/2 Desktop - Tree View

Now open the Desktop directory from the directory tree. A window that's identical to your Desktop appears on the screen. This window is very large. First go to the title bar and move the window down. Then minimize the window. Now you have a second Desktop in tree format.

HINT

Don't change this directory. If you do make changes, the Workplace Shell will no longer function properly.

From this example, you can see why OS/2 2.1 doesn't have program groups. They are no longer necessary because you can work directly with the directories.

You could use the same process under Windows, but there would be one big disadvantage. You would have to copy all the programs to such a directory in their original form. This, in turn, would use a large amount of disk space because there would be double copies of all the programs.

Developers solved this problem in OS/2 2.1 by introducing shadows. Only shadows are placed in a directory. So a directory, which contains all the programs without occupying space on the hard drive, is created.

If you display the shadows in *Details View*, you'll see that they don't have *Real Names*. You won't see anything by using DIR from the command line either. The Workplace Shell saves the shadows, which are the contents of the directories, in the extended attributes of the directory.

3.7 Settings

The *Settings* submenu item is located in every Object menu under *Open*. This choice contains all the parameters for a particular object.

The settings always appear in a notebook. This is a new screen element, which doesn't have a counterpart in Windows. In Windows, either all the information is presented in one window, or you combine the different windows into a single menu. The notebook is an object that definitely makes it easier to use the computer.

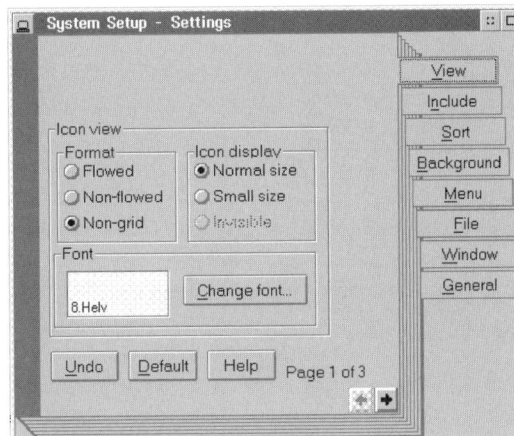

Settings Notebook

To browse through various sections of the notebook, select the tabbed dividers.

Some sections have more than one page. If this is the case, *Page x of n* appears on the pages. Use the two arrows in the lower-right corner to browse through these pages. After you browse through all the pages of one section, the arrows take you to the next section.

The ⸢Undo⸥ button restores the original status of the screen and the ⸢Help⸥ button displays information about this window.

To close a notebook, double-click the window's Title-bar icon.

You'll also find two sections, called *Window* and *General*, in every notebook. However, these two sections are different for some of the objects.

Window

The settings in the *Window* section determine the behavior of the application's window. In *Minimized button behavior*, you can determine how the window will behave when minimized. In OS/2 you can minimize a window the same way you would under Windows. Click the minimize button, the first icon to the right of the window title.

Hide window causes the window to disappear from the screen. An icon doesn't appear on the screen. The window is displayed only in the *Window List*. You can also place it on the screen by double-clicking it in the Window List. To display the *Window List*, either press ⌐Ctrl⌐ + ⌐Esc⌐ or click both mouse buttons simultaneously.

The *Minimize window to viewer* setting places the icons in the window of the same name. This is another feature that isn't available in Windows. The *Minimized Window Viewer* is a normal window that contains the icons of the minimized windows. This is useful, for example, for the programs from the *Startup* folder. Why should the FAX software continuously occupy space on your desktop. You know that it is automatically loaded and runs constantly.

With the *Minimize window to desktop setting*, everything behaves like Windows. The icons are stored on the desktop.

Windows doesn't have anything that corresponds to *Object open behavior*. It's impossible to start some applications twice under Windows. Usually you either receive an error message, such as "This application is already running", or nothing happens. Sometimes the running application is placed in the foreground.

If the *Create new window* button is active, the object will be opened a second time. It doesn't matter whether it is only a directory window appearing a second time or an application that's loaded twice.

WARNING

Not all applications run smoothly if they are started several times. Some programs have swap files that overlap and others believe that they are running in the network.

Selecting *Display existing window* places the open window of an application in the foreground.

General

The name and the icon of the program are located in this section. Enter the name of the program under *Title*. This name then appears in the corresponding directory window. The title can consist of several lines.

WARNING

> This isn't the real name of the file.

The current icon is displayed under *Current Icon*. Use (Edit) to edit the icon. To do this, select (Edit) which loads the *Icon Editor* and opens the current icon. To exit the *Icon Editor*, simply save the changed icon and close its window. The new icon is then accepted in *Current Icon*.

The (Create another) button also loads the *Icon Editor*. However, the default icon of the object appears. If it is an OS/2 or Windows program, this is the same icon as the program. If the object doesn't have its own icon, the appropriate default icon is used.

Programs

This setting contains various information about executing a program. Information about where the program is located and which data files it's associated with is also provided.

WARNING

> If you added a program to a directory as a shadow or program template, all the information won't be provided by this setting.

Program

The *Program* page contains three fields. The name of the EXE file and its path appear after *Path and Filename*. This entry is always required.

You can pass parameters to the program under *Parameters*. These parameters are added to the program call. For example, you could add the name of a source text to a call for Turbo Pascal so the source text automatically opens with Turbo Pascal.

The directory you specify under *Working Directory* will be active when the program starts. You could use this to replace program start batch files such as:

```
C:
CD \TURBO\SOURCES
..\BIN\TURBO %1 %2
```

The [Find] button activates the *Find* window. We discussed this button in the section on drive windows.

Session

The *Session* section specifies the environment in which the program is running. Only certain settings are allowed. For example, if you entered a DOS program, you cannot have it running as a WIN-OS/2-full-screen.

If *Start minimized* is active, the program is started and immediately placed on the screen as an icon.

The *Close window on exit* option closes the window immediately after exiting the program. We recommend this for most programs. However, some programs write information to the screen and exit immediately afterwards. For example, the DOS commands MEM and CHKDSK do this. To prevent OS/2 from immediately closing the window, disable this button. Then you must close the window manually.

The DOS settings are discussed in Chapter 5 and the Windows settings are discussed in Chapter 6. There are no settings for OS/2 programs.

Association

Associations of programs and their data are managed in this section. In Windows, this is done by making an entry under [Extensions] in the WIN.INI file or through the File Manager and linking.

You'll find a list of the predefined object types under *Available types*. This is useful for working with templates. We'll discuss templates later in this chapter.

Enter filenames in the *New Name* field. Then select [Add > >] to add them to the *Current Names* field. The Workplace Shell provides a connection for the entries in the *Current Names* field. This is similar to association in Windows. When you execute a data file, the associated program is started with the corresponding data.

You can enter either single files here or file masks. You can also use the wildcards * and ?.

Use ⎡<< Remove⎤ to delete entries from *Current Names*. This cancels the association.

When you double-click an associated data object to open it, the application automatically loads along with it. You could also select *Open* from the Object menu. All the applications associated with this file will appear. The small check mark in front of one of the entries indicates the default entry. This is the entry that's executed after you double-click the object.

WARNING

> It's easy to associate a file type with several programs. All the programs are then listed beneath one another in the *Open* menu. By default, the program you associated first will be executed.

In Windows it's only possible to associate a file with one program because Windows browses through the list in the WIN.INI file from the beginning and uses the first appropriate entry. Any subsequent entries are ignored.

To change the default program, open the Object menu of the corresponding data object. Then choose the *Menu* section in *Open/Settings*. Select the *Open* entry in the *Available menus* field. The button can now be selected and displays a small window. Select one of the programs under *Default Action* and then close the *Settings* window.

If you use one of the predefined object types, you must ensure that the data objects are of the same type. This involves either creating one from the appropriate template or setting the object type manually.

Type

This is where you set the object type. Then you can associate it with another application.

The object types predefined by the system are listed under *Available Types*. Select ⎡Add >>⎤ to add them to the *Current types* field.

Use ⎡<< Remove⎤ to delete an entry from *Current types*.

Menu

This page is explained later in the section on the templates.

File

The *File* section has three pages. The path and name of the directory are displayed in the *Physical Name* field under *Path* and *Name*. You cannot change this information.

Page 2 provides some information about the file. The extended attributes of the object are displayed at the top. You cannot change these attributes. The size of the object is displayed below this. You cannot modify this setting either.

The *Read only, Hidden, System,* and *Archive* flags are normal DOS file attributes. You can modify these attributes by clicking the buttons.

Entry fields are located on page 3. You can specify some information about the object under *Comments*. Under *Key phrases*, you can type some key phrases about the object. Then, when you want to search for this file, you can enter these phrases in the *Find* window. For example, you could specify the project name to which the object belongs.

You cannot modify the *History* field. An application can enter a comment or other information about the object here. For example, a Revision Control System could document the edits here.

Window

The behavior of the application is determined here. Refer to *Window* earlier in this section.

General

The name of the program and its icon are listed here. Besides the previously described options, you'll also find the *Template* option button. Use this button to declare a template for an object. See the section on templates for more information.

Directories

All the settings for influencing the appearance and contents of a directory window are located here. Since program groups are also directories, the settings are identical.

View

You modify the appearance and arrangement of icons in a window under *View*. The *View* section has three pages, which correspond to the three views of a window: *Icon view*, *Tree view*, and *Details view*.

In *Icon view* you can change the display of the icons under *Icon display*. *Normal size* displays the icons in their full size. *Small size* reduces the icons and *Invisible* hides the icons. *Format* is used to specify the position of the icons. The *Flowed* button aligns the icons on a grid (i.e., they are aligned both horizontally and vertically). The *Non-flowed* button displays the icons beneath one another. *Non-grid* arranges the icons next to one another, depending on their height and width. Use *Font* to change the font used in the object title.

Page 2 contains the settings for the *Tree view*. The *Icon display* settings are the same as in *Icon view*. The *Format* field allows you to select whether connecting lines are to be displayed in the directory tree.

The settings for *Details View* are more extensive and powerful. You can specify which details you want to display about the individual objects.

You can also change the settings for each object type individually. To do this, choose the type under *Object type* and select which data you want displayed under *Details to display*.

Under *Font* you can change the font used in the *Details* window.

Include

This is a display filter. If you enter a file mask under *Name*, only the objects, whose titles match this mask, will be displayed. For example, this is very useful for project directories. Each program has a *.CPP file and several *.h and *.res files. You can obtain an overview of all the important files and ignore the rest.

You can also specify an object type. When you set the object type under *Type*, only that object type will be displayed.

The first *Include* page permits only a rough filtering based on object title and object types. On the second page, however, you can define filters that use the attributes of the individual objects.

To add a new filter, choose (Add). A new window appears. Set the attribute to be compared under *Property to be compared*.

Set the comparison value in the *Comparison value* field. The attribute is compared with this value. You can make settings that influence the way the two values are compared in the *Comparison type* field. The *Use of criteria* field allows you to specify if the objects must match all the criteria (*AND - included objects must have criteria*) or if the object must only match one of the criteria (*OR - include objects which match criteria*).

Sort

The *Sort* page is used to determine what is included in the *Sort* pop-up menu on the Object menu. The *Object* field displays the object that can be sorted. The *Sort by attribute* field displays the attributes that can be used as sort criteria, this will vary depending on the object.

Default sort attribute allows you to set the default sorting criteria in the *Sort* pop-up menu. The *Always maintain sort order* check box lets you specify if the objects are to be sorted automatically when the window is opened.

Background

In the Background page you can determine what appears in the background of a directory. A picture or a color can be used as the background. Select one of these under *Background type*.

The [Change color] button of the *Color* setting displays the normal color wheel. Otherwise, the [Change color] button is disabled.

Use the cross-hair pointer to search for a color in this color wheel. The slider shows the current color with various brightness settings. If you enable the *Solid color* option, only solid colors are displayed in the slider. Use the [Values >>] button to display the RGB and HSB values of the current color.

If the *Background* type button is set to *Image*, the *Image* section of the window is accessible. The existing bitmaps are displayed under *File*. The bitmaps are in the C:\OS2\BITMAP directory. If you select one of these bitmaps, it will be used as a background for the window.

The [Create another] button creates a new bitmap and prepares it for editing. [Edit] is used to edit the current bitmap. Select [Find] to display the normal *Find* window. You can use this window to search for bitmaps.

Select *Normal Image* in the *Display* field to display the bitmap as it appears on the hard drive (i.e., the borders aren't filled in). Select *Tiled image* to fill the window with multiple copies of the picture. If you select *Scaled image*, the window is filled with the picture and, unlike with *Tiled image*, the image is also scaled in relation to the size of the window.

Menu

We'll discuss this page and its options in the section on Templates.

File

The *File* section also has three pages. The *Subject* field allows you to enter a brief description about the object. The *Find* procedure can then be used to search for specific subjects.

The path and name of the directory in the *Physical Name* field is displayed under *Path* and *Name*. You cannot change these settings.

The *Work Area* option is especially useful. As you already know, the Desktop is a directory. However, this directory has been declared a Work Area.

The Desktop also has some special properties. If you close the Desktop, all the programs and directories stored on it are closed. The next time you start the Desktop, the programs and directories are opened again.

You can use the *Work Area* option to assign these properties to any directory. This is similar to opening a new (small) Desktop. Doing this is especially helpful for large projects. Place all the programs and files that you'll need for a project in such a folder. When you open it, your usual working environment appears. When you close the folder, the entire *Work Area* remains in its current state. You can place everything in such a *Work Area*, including specially configured printers, custom-mapped network drives, or special templates.

The settings for page 2 and 3 are the same as the *File* settings for programs, which were already discussed.

Window

Use *Button appearance for windows* to define what happens if you minimize the object window. If you select *Hide button*, the window disappears. Under *Minimized window behavior* you can determine what happens when the minimize button is selected. You can minimize a window just as you would in Windows, by clicking the inside of the two icons next to the window title.

Other than that, the same options that are used for normal window settings are used here.

Desktop

Click the right mouse button on the empty Desktop to display the Object menu of the Desktop. Select the *Open/Settings* menu item to display the setting for the OS/2 Desktop. All the settings that are displayed for normal directories are also displayed here.

WARNING | Do not disable the *Work Area* button.

Lockup

This section contains the screen saver and an option for temporarily locking your computer. For example, you can lock the system if you must leave your computer for a while and don't want anyone to use it while you're gone.

The *Timeout* section is on the first page. Choose *No automatic lockup* to switch off the lockup. Selecting *Automatic lockup* enables the timeout lock. When this lock is active, Timeout locks up the system the number of specified minutes after the last keyboard or mouse input. This means that the screen is cleared and both keyboard and mouse are locked. So it's no longer possible to input anything and you cannot see what you were just working on.

If you switch off *Automatic lockup*, you can still use the Object menu of the Desktop to lock the system.

To unlock the computer, simply type the password. This is input on page 3. You're prompted to type the password twice so you don't make a mistake that would lock you out of your own computer.

Choose a password that's easier to remember. When you enter the password, only the cursor moves; the characters you type aren't displayed.

On page 2 you can define the appearance of the screen when the computer is locked. If you set *Display* to *Partial screen*, then only an entry line for the password appears. No other changes are made to the screen. The screen saver isn't active in this mode.

The screen behaves according to the following options with *Full Screen*. In this mode, the screen saver is also active.

The existing pictures are displayed in *File*. The pictures are in the C:\OS2\BITMAP directory. If you select one of these pictures, it will be used as a background for the window.

The [Create another] button creates a new picture and prepares it for editing. [Edit] is used to edit the current picture.

Select *Normal Image* in the *Size* field to display the bitmap as it appears on the hard drive (i.e., the borders aren't filled in).

Select *Tiled image* to fill the window with multiple copies of the picture. Selecting *Scaled image* also fills the window with the picture. However, with *Tiled image*, the picture isn't scaled; it simply fills up the entire window.

Data object

These settings are important only for data objects that weren't created from the templates. The templates pass on their characteristics to their successors. The README file on drive C: is an example of a data object.

Type

Set the object type here. You can then associate it with another application.

The object types predefined by the system are listed under *Available types*. Select (Add > >) to add them to the *Current types* field.

Use (< < Remove) to delete an entry from the *Current types* field.

Menu

A description of this page and its options are located in the section on Templates.

3.8   Shredder

The *Shredder* is the trash can of the OS/2 system. If you want to delete an object, drag it to the *Shredder*.

WARNING The *Shredder* deletes both physically and logically.

You cannot delete the *Shredder*. To remove the *Shredder* from the screen, place it in another directory.

An object will be deleted whether you copy an object to the *Shredder* or drag it there.

When you delete a shadowed file, the original remains intact; this also applies to its shadowed copies. When you delete an original file that has shadowed files, all its copies are deleted as well.

If you accidentally delete a file, you can retrieve it at the OS/2 command line with the UNDELETE command.

3.9   Templates

In this section we'll discuss how to create new objects.

Suppose that you have some folders and a pad of paper and that you want to create a new document. First you would get a folder and a sheet of paper. Then you would place the paper in the folder and write a label on the folder. Now you've created a new document (an object).

Templates are similar to a supply of empty folders and blank paper; they are empty objects. So, when you need a new object, you can use a template.

Templates folder

The templates are stored in a folder (directory) called *Templates*. This folder is on the Desktop because it's frequently used.

Open the *Templates* folder. This folder contains several objects, including programs, folders, bitmaps, and icons. You can create an object if you need one that isn't in the folder.

Using Templates

To create a new object, open the *Templates* folder and the target folder. Now simply drag the most suitable template into the target folder. This places a new (empty) object in the target folder.

HINT

> You must move the template in order to obtain an empty object. Simply copying the template creates a new template in the target folder instead of an empty object.

Templates

Templates folder

Although you've moved the template, it's still located in the *Template* folder. This is similar to the pad of paper we previously used as an example. Tearing off one sheet of paper, doesn't mean that the entire pad disappears. The template is similar to the pad of paper, and the new object is similar to the sheet of paper.

HINT

> The drive symbols in the *Drives* folder of the *OS/2 System* group aren't templates, even though they may behave like templates. These symbols are located in their folder regardless of how many times you move them around. So it isn't possible to create a new Drives object; only a shadow file is created.

HINT

> Templates cannot be deleted by dragging the object to the *Shredder*. We'll discuss how to delete them later.

A template generates an empty object. The term "empty" means that the object doesn't have any attributes except the ones included with it. At the very least, a program object must contain the name of the .EXE file. Because of this, the settings notebook for the new object appear on the desktop as soon as you launch the program.

HINT

> The new objects use their object types as a title. So you should rename the objects immediately after setup.

To do this, hold down the [Alt] key while clicking on the text under the icon. The text immediately changes to an input window. Now you can enter the new name in this window. To make the window accept the new name, click on the area surrounding the icon.

The Object menu item *Create another* also provides a way to set up an empty object. Whenever the Workplace Shell can determine the type of the current object, it will provide only the appropriate type. Otherwise, the Workplace Shell offers you all the new templates you've created. Selecting one sets up the corresponding object.

Creating templates

The *Templates* folder contains many predefined templates. However, you can also create your own templates.

Most likely you'll want to create templates for all of your old DOS applications. Templates are already supplied for OS/2 2.1

applications. However, you may also want to create new templates for these applications.

To create a new template, first select an empty object. Any object is suitable, as long as you don't pick a program or a directory. You must select a data object. The new object will be returned to the *Template* folder immediately. So you must enlarge the window to make room for it.

For example, let's create a template for a Pascal source. First select the template labeled *Data file*. Place the mouse on the icon and hold down the right mouse button. Now drag the icon to a free area in the *Template* folder.

You have created an empty object in this location. Open the Object menu of the new object. Then select *Open/Settings*; you'll return to the familiar notebook again.

On the first page, labeled *Type*, the current type of the object is given under the heading *Current Types*. Select *Plain Text*. Delete the type with `<< Remove`. Now select *Pascal Code* from *Available types* and add it using `Add >>`.

Select the page labeled *Menu*. Under *Available Menus*, select the item *Open*. Now the button labeled *Create another...* in the lower group is available. This button displays a new window.

HINT

> A tilde (~) appearing in front of a letter indicates the letter is used as a hot key for the corresponding item. This letter will also be underlined in the menu.

Enter the name of the new object under *Menu item name*. For our example, the name is *Turbo Pascal*. Under *Name*, enter the path of the .EXE file that starts Turbo Pascal.

On our computer this appears as follows:

```
C:\USR\TP601\BIN\TURBO.EXE
```

Close this window by clicking on `OK`. If you don't have Turbo Pascal on your system, enter E.EXE which will load the OS/2 System text editor.

Again, select the *Settings* switch from the upper group. The highlight bar must remain on the *Open* item. In the window that now appears, select *Turbo Pascal* under *Default action*. Close the window by clicking `OK`.

We'll explain why this page is labeled *Menu* shortly. It's easier to demonstrate the effect when the template is complete.

To convert the entire object into a template, activate the switch, *Template* on the *General* page. Now, close the notebook. The new template is assigned its typical template icon. To give your new template the proper name, rename it now.

To do this, hold down the [Alt] key and click on the text under the icon. The text changes into an entry window, in which you can enter the new name. In this example, Pascal Source would be an appropriate name.

To test the new template, follow the description on how to run a new object by using a template.

At this point the purpose of the *Menu* page should be obvious. A new menu item appears in the Object menu under the heading *Open/Turbo Pascal*, and this item is marked with a check mark as the default action. Whenever you open this object with a double-click, you launch Turbo Pascal (or the OS/2 System Editor) and transfer the source text to it as a parameter.

Perhaps you're wondering why this process is so special. Under Windows you can do all the above by creating associations. Although this is true, Windows uses wildcards to do this. So, to associate the source text with the compiler, you must make an association between the compiler and all *.PAS files. This means that ALL *.PAS files would be associated with the compiler, which creates a situation that may cause problems.

To clearly explain this, we'll use MS-WORD as an example. WORD document files have .DOC as extension, but not all .DOC files belong to WORD. Often .DOC files are pure ASCII files. In this case, it's impossible to use the extension to precisely identify a file. As a result, Windows would launch the wrong program.

The Workplace Shell, however, allows you to associate all .DOC files with the Notepad. When you open a .DOC file, the Workplace Shell immediately knows whether you're calling a WORD file. If you aren't, it loads the Notepad.

Templates that you want to create don't need to originate in the *Data File* template. You can use any other data object. You could transfer this data object from a *Drives* window into the *Templates* folder.

This data object can already contain data. For example, with your word processor you can create a letter that contains only your return address. Once you create a template with this blank letter, you can easily begin a new letter, that's ready for typing any time, by simply clicking the mouse.

Deleting templates

You cannot drag a template onto the *Shredder*. If you do this, only the object is deleted because the template itself continues to exist in its directory.

To delete a template you must switch off the *Template* switch in the *Settings* on the page marked *General*. By doing this, the template is returned to the status of a normal data object that you can then delete.

Associations between objects

Although the associations between objects are an excellent idea, you must handle them carefully.

You can associate the old DOS files with their applications just as you do in Windows. Open the Object menu of the program and select the *Open/Settings* menu item. Insert the appropriate file masks of the corresponding application (.EXE file), in the *Association* page, under the heading *Current names*.

For more information about this process, refer to *Association* in Section 3.7.

3.10 Command Line

Because OS/2 2.1 is a genuine, independent operating system, it contains its own command line interface that's very similar to the DOS interface.

Command Prompts

To activate the command line shell, open the *Command Prompts* folder in the *OS/2 System* program group.

The icons *OS/2 Window* and *OS/2 Full Screen* are located in this folder. By double-clicking on one of these icons, you can access the command line, either in window or full screen mode.

You can easily use *DOS Window* or *DOS Full Screen*. You'll see a DOS window, in which only COMMAND.COM is running. This window actually isn't needed because you can continue to run DOS programs from the OS/2 Shell.

Status line

A status line always appears above the command lines at the top of the screen. This line indicates in which operating mode you're working.

You can switch this line on or off by typing:

```
HELP OFF / ON
```

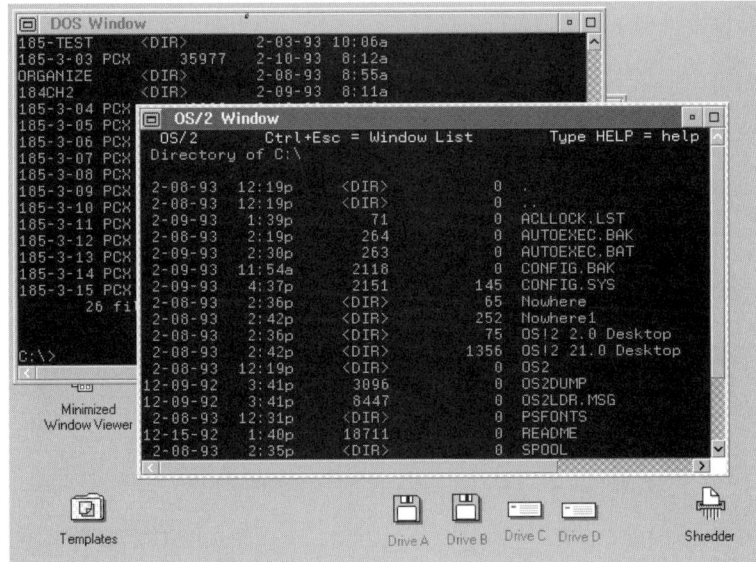

DOS Window and OS/2 Window Command Prompts

HELP

The HELP command can be very useful. Help provides explanations of the OS/2 commands and error messages.

When you encounter an error message, HELP provides a detailed explanation of what went wrong and also suggestions on how to correct the error.

So you don't have to type in the entire text of an error message, each error message also has a number. This number is always located in front of the actual message.

You must type this number as a parameter. For example:

```
HELP 21
```

You can eliminate both the leading zeros and the SYS. With the following:

```
HELP DIR
```

you receive an explanation of the DIR command, which includes all its parameters. To do this, HELP activates the OS/2 2.1 *Command Reference* program.

It's also possible to display only an overview of the parameters. To do this, type:

```
DIR /?
```

Compatibility

Working with the OS/2 Shell is very similar to working with DOS. However, remember that OS/2 is a multitasking system.

If you receive an error message regarding access to a device or a file, always first determine whether another program is using this device or file.

You can continue to use most commands, such as DIR, COPY, XCOPY, FORMAT, CD, etc., as before. Also, you can use DOS programs without any problems. OS/2 2.1 recognizes these programs and opens a DOS window for them.

Ending a session

To exit the command line Shell use EXIT, as under DOS.

A faster way to exit the Shell is by simply closing its window. However, try not to use this method because it may cause problems for your system.

Chapter 4

—— Help In OS/2 2.1 ——

One of the most important aspects of a modern operating system is a comprehensive online help system. Under Windows, this help system is part of its basic design. OS/2 has taken this design a step farther, since help is available any time and for every object.

Although DOS 6.0 contains an overview of possible parameters required by the commands, a comprehensive help system still isn't available at the DOS level.

Complete documentation is a basic component of UNIX systems. This is obviously very important for complicated systems such as UNIX. Because these systems are so complex and comprehensive, it isn't possible to use a manual for documentation because it would be extremely large.

OS/2 2.1 also includes a modern help system for the complete Workplace Shell, all the applications accompanying the system, and, of course, the command line interface.

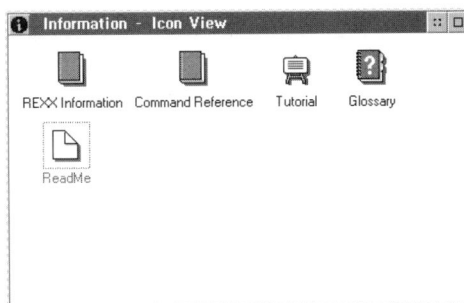

Help folder

Help programs are located either on the Desktop, *Master Help Index* and *Start Here* programs, or in the *Information* directory. The *Information* directory contains the *REXX Information*, *Command Reference, Tutorial, Glossary* programs and a ReadMe file.

To activate Help, press ⎡F1⎤. Under OS/2 2.1, every option and every object has its own help. The entire help system is based on only two programs. One program works like a manual and the other is a hypertext system.

The same help program is used in the *Master Help Index* and in the *Glossary*, but it uses a different database. In the same way, the *Command Reference* and the *REXX Information* help systems have a similar structure and operation.

4.1   Tutorial

The Tutorial introduces you to the Workplace Shell and how it operates. If you know how to use a mouse, you can easily use this program.

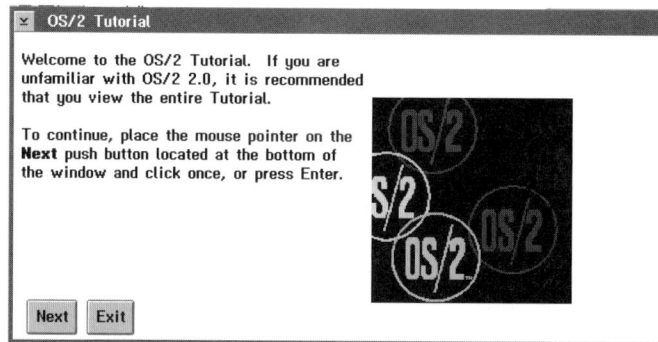

OS/2 Tutorial

Welcome to the OS/2 Tutorial. If you are unfamiliar with OS/2 2.0, it is recommended that you view the entire Tutorial.

To continue, place the mouse pointer on the **Next** push button located at the bottom of the window and click once, or press Enter.

Next   Exit

OS/2 Tutorial program

4.2   Start Here

The help database *Start Here* provides help for the most important and most frequently asked questions. If you've switched from another operating system, you'll find answers to many questions, such as "How do I use my old programs?", "How do I use the Workplace Shell?", and "How do I install my printer?".

Various subject groups are located under the heading *Contents*. Double-click on one of these items to display its explanation in the right half of the window.

All the explanation texts are also linked to one another. Additional explanations are available for each of the

highlighted entries. You can display these by double-clicking on
them.

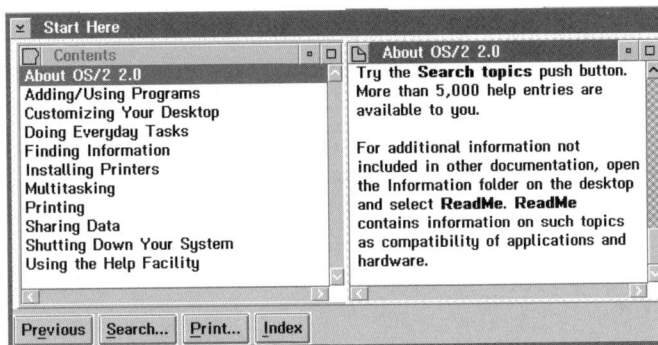

Start Here help program

The button marked (Previous) allows you to move backwards through
the help pages. When you reach the first help page, another click
on this button closes help and returns you to the previous screen.

The button marked (Index) displays the key word directory. You can
access additional help from here also.

Search

The (Search...) button displays a search window. Enter the search
information under the *Search for* heading. The buttons below
determine where the search should be performed. The radio
buttons *Marked Sections* and *Marked Libraries* enable you to limit
the search. To begin this search, click on the chapters you want to
search and then click on (Search...).

Once found, the pages are displayed in a window that also lists
the titles of the corresponding help pages. Double-clicking on
these texts displays the text that belongs with them. The item
searched for will be highlighted in the texts in a different color.

Printing

The (Print...) button prints the help documentation on the default
printer. After selecting this button, another window appears. In
this window you can determine what should be printed.

4.3   Command Reference

The *Command Reference* provides an overview of all the OS/2 2.1 command line commands. This includes both DOS and OS/2 2.1 commands. Also, it displays all drivers and information about CONFIG.SYS.

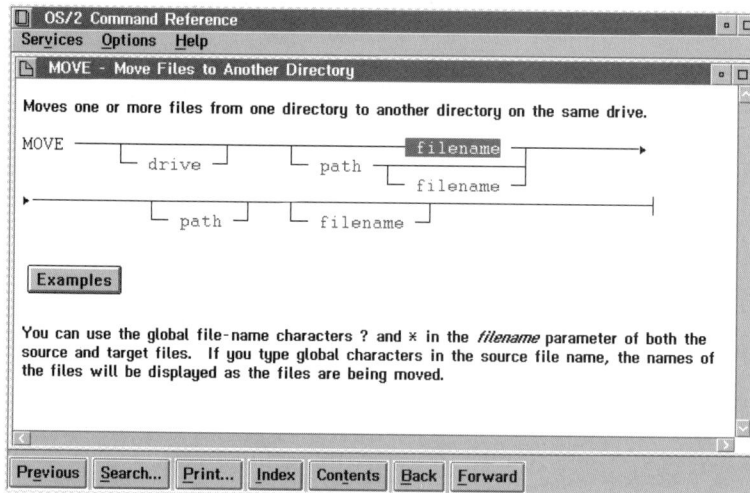

Command Reference

You can activate the *Command Reference* in two ways.

Command Line

When you're at the command line, you can use the HELP command to receive help.

Simply add the appropriate information to the command. For example, entering HELP DIR displays the help page for the DIR command.

Workplace Shell

The *Command Reference* help program is also located in the *Information* folder on the Desktop.

Finding Information

When the program starts, you'll be located in the uppermost level. There are two ways to find a command in the *Command Reference*.

The first is *OS/2 Commands by Name* which is an alphabetical list of all commands. The second is *OS/2 Commands by Task Category* which lists all commands according to task types.

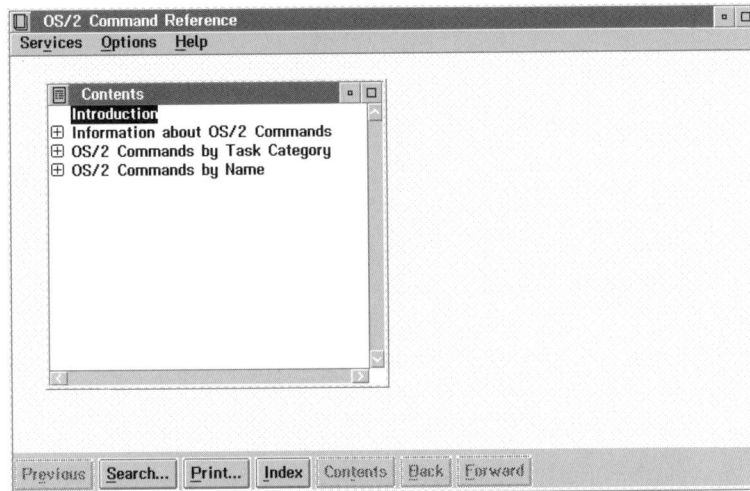

OS/2 Command Reference

An addition sign (+) appears in front of both items. This works the same way as the addition sign (+) in the directory tree. Use this sign to open the level immediately below. Then the addition sign changes to a subtraction sign that closes the tree again. You can also use *Expand branch* and *Collapse branch* in the *Options* menu to perform these tasks.

Then double-click on one of the entries. The help page that appears contains the desired information. Linked items are highlighted in a different color. Double-clicking on a linked item will display help about the item.

A syntax diagram for every command is presented first. This diagram shows all the parameters possible for any command. By double-clicking on them, an explanation for each parameter appears.

Each button also contains an [Examples] button. This button displays a page with examples and explanations for the command. Select the [Contents] button to return to the directory index. To see a list of all the help pages that have been displayed, select *Viewed pages* in the *Options* menu. The [Back] and [Forward] buttons flip through the help database page by page.

Storing

You don't always have to print a help page. To save the information in a file, select the menu items *Copy, Copy to file,* and *Append to file* from the *Services* menu.

Copy copies the help page into a temporary file. You can process it further with another application. *Copy to file* copies the help page to a file called TXT.TMP in the current directory. Copying to this file means that any previous information the file contained is deleted. However, *Append to file* adds the current help page to this file. The program automatically creates this file if it doesn't already exist.

Bookmark

By selecting *Bookmark* from the *Services* menu you can create or search for a bookmark. The bookmark window displays all other available bookmarks. You can jump to any marked page by double-clicking on the appropriate bookmark.

By using bookmarks, you can create your own index.

4.4   REXX Information

Here you'll find information about working with REXX and a complete REXX reference guide.

REXX Information is similar to the *OS/2 Command Reference*. Look here for help for any problems you may encounter with REXX.

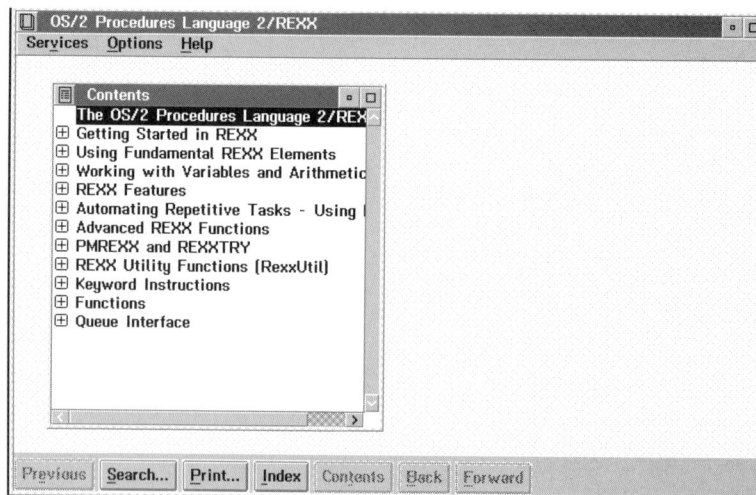

OS/2 Tutorial program

4.5   Master Help Index

The *Master Help Index* resembles a book with tabs. This program
is based on keywords. A long list appears containing all the
possible keywords. You can obtain explanations about each
keyword. Even the explanations given here are linked to each
other.

Master Help Index

The *Glossary* contains definitions of various terms and the *Master
Help Index* contains descriptions of actions.

Use the tabs to flip quickly through its pages. You can also use the
scroll bars to do this.

Usually, all the catalog tab letters don't fit into the window. So
you'll see two double arrow buttons above and below the tabs. Use
these buttons to flip through the letters.

You can also enter, on your keyboard, the first letter of the entry
you want to find. The cursor moves to the first item that starts
with that letter.

By clicking on ⌐Search topics¬, you can search for an item or a keyword.
Enter the item to be searched for under *Search string* and begin the
search by clicking on ⌐Search¬.

4.6   Glossary

This is a complete OS/2 glossary, which contains explanations for almost all topics in every area of the operating system and the computer in general.

The *Glossary* help section also uses a help notebook. For a description of the notebook, refer to the previous section.

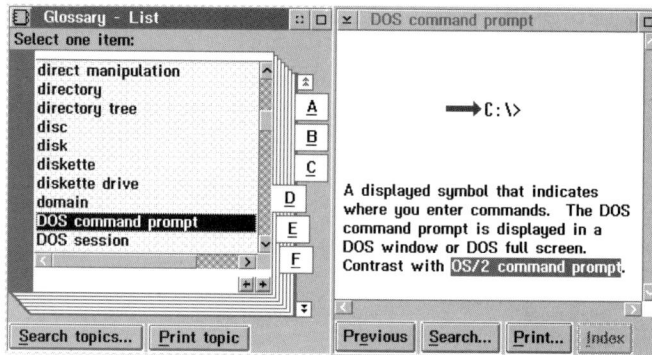

OS/2   Glossary

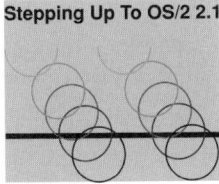

Chapter 5

—— DOS Windows ——

The older versions of OS/2 were criticized because they didn't contain DOS windows. So, IBM made some drastic changes in OS/2 2.1.

OS/2 2.1 and UNIX are the first true 32 bit operating systems for PCs. Since OS/2 2.1 was specifically designed for the 386, it's the first program that can properly use the concept of virtual machines.

WARNING

Before you install a DOS or Windows program under OS/2 2.1 for the first time, make a backup copy of your CONFIG.SYS file onto a floppy diskette. Some programs significantly change this file, which can cause problems in OS/2 2.1.

Most programs ask whether you want to alter the CONFIG.SYS file. If you cannot prevent such a change, make a copy of your CONFIG.SYS. Then you can compare it with the new (probably damaged) CONFIG.SYS and make any necessary changes manually.

If a program does change the OS/2 CONFIG.SYS file so the computer will no longer boot, you can boot using the first two installation diskettes of OS/2. When the second diskette's welcome screen appears, press [Esc] to enter the OS/2 command line. You can then copy the backup copy of your CONFIG.SYS file to the hard drive.

5.1 Launching Programs

You can easily use a regular DOS program. Simply launch the program from either the command line or the Workplace Shell. The program starts up with the default settings.

DOS programs can run in windows or in full screen mode. This also applies to text and graphics applications. To switch between these modes, press the [Alt]+[Esc] keys. It's also easy to use the mouse for any DOS program in a window.

5.2   Setting Up Programs

The easiest way to set up programs is to link programs in a program group using *Migrate*. You already learned how to do this during the installation of OS/2 2.1.

There are two ways to set up a program manually. Either create a new program object or insert a shadowed .EXE file into a program group. Although the second method is simpler, it's the less flexible approach.

If you're using work areas, the second approach is more flexible because a shadowed file always exactly matches the original. However, whenever you set up several independent programs, the settings for the individual objects are easy to configure. You can, for example, then insert separate working directories.

Use the template labeled *Program* to create an empty object in the program group. To do this, simply place the template in the appropriate window. Now you'll create a new program object. Because one field of the settings must be occupied, the *Settings* open immediately. Fill in the required settings and close the notebook. You can launch the program with a double-click. This brings us to the settings.

5.3   Settings

The settings for DOS programs correspond to the Windows PIFs. In the settings, OS/2 2.1 stores information on how to make applications run despite themselves. You may also want to provide a different operating environment for your applications.

Unlike Windows, which stores additional information in a Program Information File (PIF), the Workplace Shell stores these files under the extended attributes of each object.

To obtain the settings for any program object, activate *Open/Settings* from the *Object* menu.

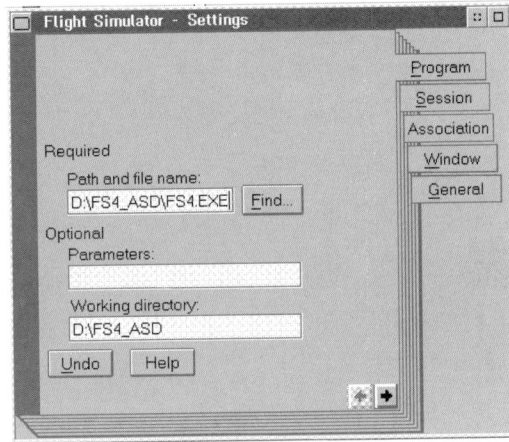

Program Settings notebook page

The first page, the *Program* section, contains information on the .EXE file itself. Under *Path and file name*, you'll see the name of the .EXE file and its path. This item is extremely important.

For example:

```
C:\USER\BORLANDC\BIN\BC.EXE
```

You can assign parameters to the program under *Parameters*. These parameters are entered after the program's filename. At this point you can also, for example, give Turbo Pascal the name of a source text that will be opened automatically when you launch the program.

The directory given under the heading *Working directory* is active when the program starts. With its help, you can replace the most frequently used program batch files, such as:

```
C:
CD \TURBO\SOURCES
..\BIN\TURBO %1 %2
```

By working with program objects instead of shadowed files, you can insert the *Parameters* and *Working Directory* items into all the objects differently. So, you can use the same compiler in several projects because it finds a different configuration file each time.

The *Session* section describes the environment in which the program is running. For the moment, you can select only the allowable settings. If you've inserted a DOS program, you cannot run it as a *Win-OS/2 full screen*.

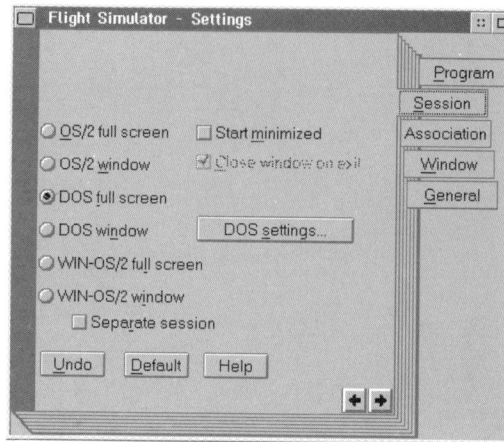

Session Settings notebook page

Activating the *Start minimized* option starts a program and minimizes its icon on the screen.

The *Close window on exit* option closes the window as soon as a program stops running. You should use this option for most programs. However, there are a few programs that write messages to the screen and then automatically terminate. The DOS commands MEM and CHKDSK are examples of this. To prevent OS/2 from immediately closing a window, you must disable this switch. Then you must close this window manually.

DOS Settings

The [DOS Settings...] button displays actual information about the DOS settings.

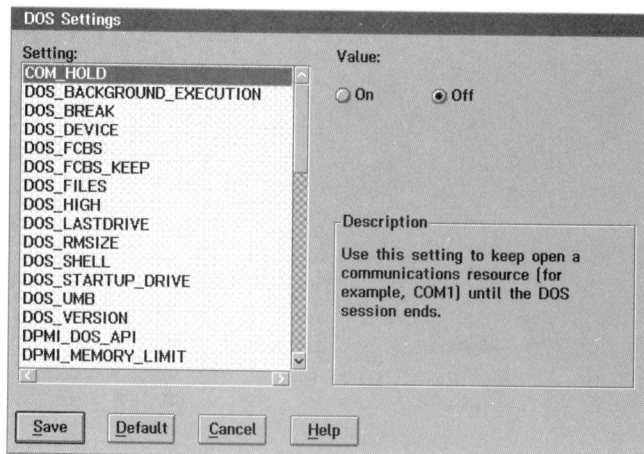

DOS Settings dialog

NOTE

Make certain the DOS windows work independently of each other. Each DOS window has its own environment, separate files, FCBS, and devices. So, the values can be much lower here because they apply to only one application at a time.

COM_Hold

This switch allows a program to maintain its access to a serial port until it's finished running.

DOS_BACKGROUND_EXECUTION

To keep a program running in the background, this switch must be activated. In Windows programs that work with DDE, this switch must also remain active.

DOS_BREAK

This is identical to the DOS BREAK command. If this switch is activated, you can abort access to the hard drive with Ctrl + C.

DOS_DEVICE

This makes it possible for you to link DOS device drivers. This item looks as follows:

```
C:\DOS\SSTOR.SYS
```

The usual beginning of the statement "DEVICE=" is eliminated. Only the driver itself and any necessary parameters are included:

```
C:\DEVS\X00.SYS 2
```

DOS_FCBS and DOS_FCBS_KEEP

These two entries match the following DOS line exactly and determine the number of File Control Blocks:

```
FCBS=DOS_FCBS , DOS_FCBS_KEEP
```

DOS_FILES

This corresponds to the entry of the same name in the DOS CONFIG.SYS.

DOS_HIGH

This matches the first parameter of the statement:

```
DOS=HIGH,UMB
```

If the UMB switch is activated, the DOS kernel is loaded into the High Memory Area.

DOS_LASTDRIVE

To install a network driver, a RAM disk, or a SuperStor drive, you must adjust this setting accordingly.

DOS_RMSIZE

This reduces the amount of memory in the DOS window. This helps you test whether your program will still run on a computer with 256 or 512 kilobytes. It forces the DOS window to use less memory.

DOS_SHELL

This setting is identical to the SHELL statement in the CONFIG.SYS. It allows you to install an alternative command processor and lets you continue to use 4DOS in the DOS window, for example.

DOS_STARTUP_DRIVE

This setting is explained in Section 5.7, Booting a DOS Window.

DOS_UMB

The entry:

```
DOS=HIGH,UMB
```

makes the Upper Memory Blocks available and loads the drivers there.

DOS_VERSION

With this setting, you can substitute an incorrect DOS version number in your programs. Under MS-DOS, SETVER handles any false version numbers.

Three numbers follow the program name. The first two are the version number, and the last one determines how often the wrong number is relayed to the program.

The following entry returns DOS Version 3.74 to the program MFT.EXE 5 times:

```
MFT.EXE,3.74,5
```

OS/2 2.1 returns DOS Version 20.00. Depending on the capacity, this is probably an accurate approximation. However, it's difficult to determine this because version numbers continue to increase. Use the VER command from the command line to verify the version number.

OS/2 1.x returns DOS Version number 10.00. This setting actually isn't important under OS/2 2.1, because the request for a version number in the programs tends to have its own logic.

Since you can boot with any DOS Version under OS/2 2.1, simply make the required DOS version available to the program. However, there are programs that aren't intended to run under OS/2 2.1. For example:

```
MSD.EXE,5,00,255
```

This item also launches the Microsoft Diagnose Tool.

DPMI_DOS_API

OS/2 2.1 is a DPMI server. With it, you can also run DOS Extenders in the DOS windows. This group includes the Borland C++ Compiler, for example.

DPMI is a further development of the older VCPI specification. VCPI isn't supported under OS/2 2.1 because it cannot guarantee the integrity of the system. Windows also supports DPMI.

Use this switch to disable the DPMI server.

DPMI_MEMORY_LIMIT

This switch sets how much memory an application can demand from the DPMI.

NOTE

> This entry is indicated in megabytes. If this value is too large, it can use too much memory.

Using more memory than is physically available doesn't present a problem either. OS/2 2.1 creates memory by using its virtual memory manager on the hard drive. However, you must ensure that enough space is available there.

DPMI_NETWORK_BUF_SIZE

If a DPMI application has difficulty accessing network drives, its buffer is probably too small. Use this setting to enlarge it.

EMS_FRAME_LOCATION

This setting determines the location of the page frame in active EMS emulation.

Auto finds a suitable area on its own and is quite reliable. With *None*, you can disable the emulation.

EMS_HIGH_OS_MAP_REGION

Here you decide how much memory the program may insert, in addition to the normal page frame, above the 640K limit. Several programs increase the page frame in this way so more memory is available at any one time.

EMS_LOW_OS_MAP_REGION

Here you can set how much re-mappable memory should be allocated to an application.

Most applications cannot use re-mappable memory because it wasn't introduced until EMS 3.2. Later the EMS 4.0 specifications absorbed it. However, usually applications still work with EMS 3.2 because genuine EMS 4.0 cards are very rare.

EMS_MEMORY_LIMIT

Use this to set the highest amount of memory that an application may access with an EMS driver.

NOTE

> This entry is indicated in kilobytes. The maximum possible is 32 Meg.

HW_NOSOUND

Switching this to ON prevents a program from accessing the internal speaker.

HW_ROM_TO_RAM

With this feature, OS/2 2.1 creates Shadow RAM that copies the contents of the ROM. Use this to increase the speed of a DOS application.

OS/2 2.1 itself cannot use Shadow RAM since it doesn't access ROM anyway.

HW_TIMER

This gives the program direct access to the computer's clock. Several time critical programs, such as terminal emulators, use this feature.

IDLE_SECONDS

This sets the elapsed time before OS/2 2.1 begins to watch a program. The idle detection isn't activated until after a specified number of seconds.

IDLE_SENSITIVY

Use this feature to determine the percentage of a program's running time that can be used for reading the keyboard.

Whenever a program is simply checking for input, it's probably waiting for something to happen. It doesn't need calculating time to do this. This slows down the program.

KBD_ALTHOME_BYPASS

By pressing [Alt] + [Home] you can switch an application between full screen and window displays.

First OS/2 2.1 and then the application evaluates every input from the keyboard. Therefore, the key combination [Alt] + [Home] doesn't reach the application at all.

If the application itself uses this key combination, however, then OS/2 2.1 will relay it, if the switch is active. Then you can use the Object menu to switch between full screen and window mode.

KBD_BUFFER_EXTEND

OS/2 2.1 uses this to create an extra keyboard buffer for an application. Such a buffer can be very helpful in a multitasking environment because it's possible, at least theoretically, that a keystroke can get lost.

KBD_CTRL_BYPASS

Use the key combinations [Ctrl]+[Esc] and [Alt]+[Esc] to switch between applications.

First OS/2 2.1 and then the application evaluates every input from the keyboard. Therefore, key combinations [Ctrl]+[Esc] and [Alt]+[Esc] aren't passed to the application at all.

If the application itself uses these keystroke combinations, you can determine which key OS/2 2.1 shouldn't evaluate. You can disable only one of these keys; otherwise you would no longer be able to switch from the application.

KBD_RATE_LOCK

This prevents an application from changing the keyboard repeat rate. A multitasking environment cannot tolerate a repeat rate that changes.

MEM_EXCLUDE_REGIONS

Here you indicate which memory areas OS/2 2.1 shouldn't use.

MEM_INCLUDE_REGIONS

OS/2 2.1 allows you to use the memory regions specified here.

MOUSE_EXCLUSIVE_ACCESS

Some programs have difficulty with the mouse emulation. Two mouse cursors will appear in their windows. Usually these cursors are displaced by the same interval. Use this switch to turn off the second mouse.

> **NOTE**
> To retrieve the Desktop mouse, press Ctrl+Esc, Alt+Esc, or simply Alt to reactivate the Desktop.

Norton Utilities' SysInfo is an example of such a program.

TOUCH_EXCLUSIVE_ACCESS

You should activate this function if you're using an IBM 8516 Touch screen. Otherwise, some problems will occur with emulation.

PRINT_TIMEOUT

Under OS/2 2.1, a program must allow the printer to be assigned to it. Then the other programs know that they must wait until the printer is no longer busy.

When a program opens a print job, OS/2 first loads the data into a spooler.

Many programs print online. This means that they calculate each line and then print it out immediately. So, access to the printer is blocked while the program is printing. That is why OS/2 2.1 spools the data out of the way and doesn't actually start to print until the program itself is finished printing. This is a better way to use the printer's capabilities.

DOS programs, however, don't switch the printer on and off. Instead, they simply print. So, OS/2 2.1 spools output, but it doesn't know when a DOS program is finished. After nothing has been loaded into the spooler for the set number of seconds, OS/2 2.1 assumes that a program is finished.

For programs that run very slowly, you may have to increase this time setting.

VIDEO_8514A_XBG_IOTRAP

You can speed up a program with this switch if you have an 8514A or an XGA. Then OS/2 2.1 doesn't reserve any memory for holding screen data when you switch programs.

Since these programs usually understand the VIDEO_SWITCH signal, they should restore the screen automatically. Then you should activate the VIDEO_SWITCH_NOTIFICATION switch.

You cannot cut any data out of the screen because OS/2 2.1 no longer has any controllers for the screen memory.

Also, you'll no longer be able to run this program from a window.

VIDEO_FASTPASTE

Some programs have trouble when the keyboard input is very fast. Whenever OS/2 2.1 moves data from the temporary buffer into a DOS program, it simulates keystrokes. OS/2 2.1 can do this faster than any person.

To keep a program from losing data when it's entered, use this switch to reduce the input speed.

VIDEO_MODE_RESTRICTION

Sometimes OS/2 2.1 indicates that a smaller graphics card than the one that's actually installed is being used.

VIDEO_ONDEMAND_MEMORY

When you switch from a full screen display, OS/2 2.1 stores the screen memory in RAM. The switch determines when to reserve the memory needed to do this.

With ON, the system reserves the memory at the moment you switch off the application. With OFF, the memory is reserved at the start of a program.

For the current resolutions and color intensities, the memory requires almost 1 Meg for such an image. If you start three such applications, they'll occupy, yet not actually use, 3 Meg in RAM.

So you can use this switch to save memory or time. If the memory isn't made available until it's needed, then it's possible that no memory is available. The system must make room by temporarily dumping the contents of other memory areas onto the hard drive.

VIDEO_RETRACE_EMULATION

With this switch, you can activate the retrace emulation, which is a feature that's needed by some programs.

This emulation costs some additional processing time. Also, with some programs it's possible that the color palette may become slightly jumbled when you switch between programs.

VIDEO_ROM_EMULATION

OS/2 2.1 captures some BIOS functions and executes them itself. This occurs only in text mode. Emulation significantly increases processing speed. If your VGA-BIOS expands these functions and your application uses them, then you must switch off this emulation feature. This feature offers only the default VGA-BIOS.

VIDEO_SWITCH_NOTIFICATION

OS/2 2.1 can send a signal to an application indicating that the program has been switched to the foreground or background. Some programs can take advantage of this signal by dumping screen data or restoring it all by themselves.

This switch allows you to turn the signal on or off.

VIDEO_WINDOW_REFRESH

For OS/2 2.1 to display a program in a window, it must read its video memory. Use this switch to determine how often this should occur.

Some programs run very slowly and don't produce a lot of video output. A good example of this is a program that performs simple calculations. Refreshing the screen every tenth of a second isn't necessary; every 30 seconds is sufficient. Using this setting saves the processor a lot of work.

The adjustment is made by tenths of seconds.

XMS_HANDLES

This setting determines how many handles the XMS handler should keep available. Generally, you won't need to change the default setting. Whenever a program can't find enough handles, it will notify you with an appropriate error message.

XMS_MEMORY_LIMIT

This feature sets the highest number of XMS blocks an application may need.

This is indicated in megabytes.

NOTE
> If you assign more memory than is physically available, the hard drive will simulate it. The program obtains its memory, but works more slowly.

XMS_MINIMUM_HMA

The High Memory Area isn't freed until the amount of memory required exceeds a certain limit.

Set this in kilobytes.

5.4   Memory Management

In the DOS windows, OS/2 2.1 provides a memory management capability that even controls all the techniques that are used under DOS. To do this, it uses an EMS-XMS emulation, the DPMI, UMBs, and HMA. DOS memory can even be extended into the Video memory area.

However, VCPI programs don't run in the DOS windows. For data security reasons, VCPI cannot be used. Because a VCPI can cause the entire computer to crash, the integrity of the system cannot be ensured.

Besides, OS/2 2.1 provides a DPMI, just as Windows does in 386 mode. You can consider the DPMI specification a further development of VCPI specification.

You'll probably find many settings that you'll never need. We'll briefly discuss the settings that are used for everyday work.

The *DPMI Memory Limit* setting is for applications that can work with DPMI. The same is true for the *EMS Memory Limit*. All your programs must be able to work with EMS memory.

Pure DOS applications are rarely able to work with XMS memory. However, there are increasingly more applications that can do this. To determine how much memory these applications can demand, use the *MXS Memory Limit*.

You should be careful with some applications. The Turbo C++ Compiler, for example, reserves all available memory for itself. So, you must control these memory-hungry applications.

Set the Video_Mode_Restriction on Mono or Color to increase DOS memory. This is possible because these cards lie further back in the address area. For a CGA card, another 96K is available and for a Mono card another 64K is available.

QEMM provides a similar feature, where VIDRAM performs a similar function. For this to work, don't decrease the RAM with DOS-RMSIZE.

Set the DOS HIGH switch to ON so you'll be able to load a program into high memory. A DOS window frees 746K. This is more than most DOS Memory Managers can do.

5.5   CONFIG.SYS

OS/2 2.1's CONFIG.SYS contains several settings that affect DOS windows.

```
BREAK, DOS, DEVICE, FCBS, FILES, LASTDRIVE, SHELL
```

These statements correspond to the statements with the same names in the DOS CONFIG.SYS.

Use these settings only when you start a program from the Workplace Shell. When you launch a program from the command line, OS/2 2.1 uses the default settings. This same procedure is used under Windows. A program can make the most of the PIF files only when you start it under the Program Manager.

When it starts, the system reads the CONFIG.SYS.

5.6   AUTOEXEC.BAT

The AUTOEXEC.BAT applies to all DOS windows. This enables
you to install a specific device driver.

Unlike the CONFIG.SYS, the AUTOEXEC.BAT is executed for
every DOS window, instead of at the system boot. Here you can use
all the programs that you've used under DOS.

You no longer need the disk protection program Mirror because
OS/2 2.1 has its own mechanism. Through its definition of the
environment variable DELDIR, OS/2 2.1 activates its own
Undelete mechanism, which is even more reliable than Mirror.

5.7   Booting a DOS Window

If a program asks for a specific DOS version, first you can try using
the DOS Version setting. If this doesn't work, you can provide the
required version. Under OS/2 2.1, you can boot a DOS window from
a diskette or a hard disk image of a diskette.

Starting a window

You can start a window with a different version of DOS. You can
even start an entire operating system in this way. (We tried this
with Minix and didn't encounter any problems.)

Insert a DOS diskette into the drive and enter this drive as the
settings for *DOS_Start_Up_Drive*. As soon as the program starts,
this window will boot from the diskette.

Exiting

You cannot quit this type of DOS version by using EXIT. DOS
thinks it's running on a normal computer. As a result, you cannot
quit the primary Shell. So you must make DOS think that you've
switched off the computer. Do this by simply closing the window.

Configuring DOS

When you try this, you'll notice that something is missing in this
DOS window. You cannot access HPFS partitions; you also don't
have a mouse or extra memory.

OS/2 2.1 uses its own drivers to solve these problems. These make
the system resources available to you in the unaccustomed DOS
windows.

The entries in the CONFIG.SYS that will handle these tasks look
as follows:

```
device=fsfilter.sys
device=himem.sys
device=emm386.sys noems
DOS=high,umb
```

The FSFilter makes HPFS disks available to you. The two drivers,
HIMEM.SYS and EMM386.SYS, retain their normal function as
under DOS.

You still must add the mouse driver to your AUTOEXEC.BAT.

```
LH MOUSE.COM
```

You can find these drivers in your directory.

```
C:\OS2\MSDOS
```

Also copy these to your DOS diskette.

Image file

You can speed up this process if you frequently use a DOS boot
diskette. To create an image file for the diskette, use the VMDISK
program.

The following command allows you to copy the entire diskette
from A: to a file called DOS33.IMG. Enter this file under DOS
start up and it immediately boots from this file:

```
VMDISK A: C:\DOS33.IMG
```

Then DOS thinks that the image file is drive A:. With this file,
you can work in the usual way. Whenever you use drive A:, you
access that file instead of the disk drive. To access the drive
again, use:

```
FSACCESS A:
```

Make certain a valid COMMAND.COM is on the diskette.

5.8   Device Drivers

You can continue to use your device drivers in the DOS windows. However, you no longer need most of the other drivers. You also don't need memory managers, mouse drivers, and disk caches.

WARNING

Don't install a cache program in a DOS window. This could cause problems because OS/2 2.1 already has its own integrated cache.

This feature is generally used for scanners or similar drivers. You should install these only for programs that use such drivers.

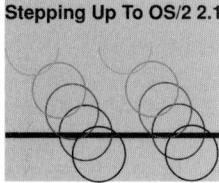

Chapter 6

Using Windows Programs

Compared to the older OS/2 versions, the migration capabilities of OS/2 2.1 have significantly improved. With OS/2 2.1 you can work directly with Windows 3.1 applications without any problems.

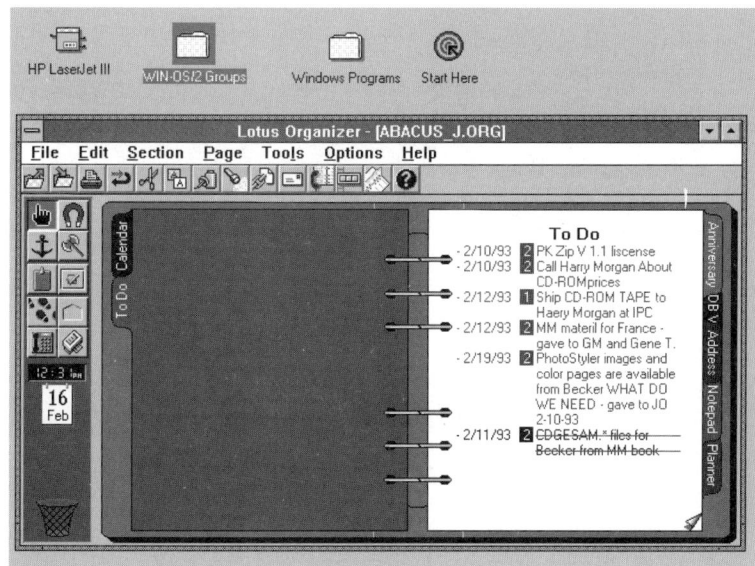

Lotus Organizer for Windows under OS/2 2.1

Since IBM uses Microsoft's source text for Windows, you don't have to worry about incompatibilities between Windows and OS/2 2.1. Unlike OS/2 2.0, OS/2 2.1 can run Windows 3.1 applications.

File swapping using the Clipboard and DDE is no problem under OS/2 2.1. This also works between applications that are running under different modes. As a result, you can transfer something from Windows' Corel Draw to a PMChart image running as an OS/2 2.1 application.

Although OS/2 2.1 can work directly with Windows applications, genuine 32-bit software is faster and has other advantages. To make program porting easier for today's developers, Micrografx, in a collaboration with IBM, provides two tools for programmers. The "Mirrors" package is responsible for program porting and "Oasis" handles device drivers. These tools automate porting to a greater or lesser degree, depending on the application.

The standard Windows 3.1 Accessories and Main groups are located in the *WIN-OS/2* and *Windows Program* folders, if you installed Windows support with OS/2.

6.1　Setting Up Programs

Using *Migrate Applications* is the easiest way to place a program in a program group. The previous chapter on DOS windows explains how to insert a program in a program group.

The settings on the *Session* page of the objects notebook determine whether the programs will run on the Desktop.

6.2　Launching Programs

To launch a program, simply start it if you're using a normal Windows program.

The default setting usually runs the programs in full screen mode on the OS/2 Desktop.

To start Windows in a full screen, type the following at the OS/2 command line:

```
WINOS2
```

This displays the regular opening screen with the Program Manager. You can then easily start a Windows application. OS/2 2.1 notices, by the EXE header, that it's working with a Windows application and will start Windows automatically.

Whenever you launch several programs from a full screen Windows, all the programs run in the same virtual machine. As a result, they can interfere with each other. If one of these applications crashes, it can cause the others to also crash.

You can start several programs in one full screen session. You can even start several full screen sessions simultaneously. It's also possible to run a full screen Windows with several programs at the same time as a Windows application in Seamless mode. This produces a situation that isn't possible under Windows: Several different Windows are running on one computer.

Because these virtual Windows machines don't know about each other, each one manages its own buffer. However, this isn't very practical.

OS/2 provides a *Public Clipboard* that's available for all Windows machines. At this point you can decide whether a Windows machine should be included on this *Clipboard*.

This is setup using the *WIN-OS/2 Setup* application located in the System Setup folder. Select the WIN-OS/2 Setup application and then the Data Exchange page of the notebook. Select *Public (share with WIN-OS/2)*. When it's active, the session uses the *Public Clipboard*; otherwise it manages its own *Clipboard*.

6.3   Settings

These settings are identical to the DOS settings. Only three switches have been added.

WIN_RUNMODE

This switch determines the Windows operation mode. You can set this to *Auto*, *Real*, or *Standard*.

With the *Real* setting, OS/2 2.1 can run old Windows 2.x applications, which is something Windows 3.1 cannot do. With *Auto*, the program uses the highest mode in which it can still run. The *Standard* setting forces the program to run in Windows 3 protected mode.

WIN_DDE

This switch allows Windows to share DDE information with other public Windows and OS/2 sessions. It can be set to *On* or *Off*.

WIN_CLIPBOARD

This switch allows Windows to share Clipboard information with other public Windows and OS/2 sessions. It can be set to *On* or *Off*.

6.4   Windows Device Drivers

Under OS/2 2.1, you can continue to use the regular Windows 3 device drivers. The printer driver is then available for all Windows applications; the video drivers, however, are available only in the full screen mode.

You must insert the video drivers into the SYSTEM.INI file manually because the Windows *SetUp* no longer provides the video setting. See your Windows documentation for more information.

You set up a printer driver in the usual way - using the *Control Panel* of the Program Manager. You can find the tool for it in the Program Manager whenever you start Windows in full screen mode.

Use one of the LPTx.OS2 files to install the printer driver.

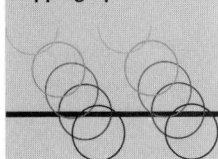

Chapter 7

Multitasking and File Swapping

The new OS/2 2.1 turns your computer into a true multitasking power machine.

7.1 Multitasking Basics

Since today's computers are so powerful, they are rarely overloaded. A modern AT spends over 95% of its life waiting for the next keystroke. However, you can use this idle time if the operating system permits multitasking. This is possible with OS/2 2.1.

Multitasking means that several programs or processes run simultaneously. Suppose that you start a long process (sorting a database, printing a long document, etc.) or a program that takes a long time to complete a task (backing up, formatting a diskette, etc.). Under OS/2 2.1 you can simply use this time to do something else with the computer. For example, look at new programs, continue working on a document, enter new items into a database, or play a game.

Some multitasking is possible under Desqview or Windows. However, OS/2 2.1 provides true multitasking. There are many reasons why OS/2 2.1 has this capability. A major reason is that instead of being created from the old DOS, OS/2 contains its own functions.

Multitasking: in the background

You may be wondering whether you actually need multitasking. However, once you've worked with OS/2 for awhile, you'll wonder how you ever managed without it. Working with your computer becomes much easier and productive.

7.2   Launching Several Programs

To experience multitasking, first you must launch several programs. Start these programs simply by double-clicking on their icons.

NOTE	To conserve working memory, allot your DOS applications only as much memory as they need. Use DOS Settings to do this.

Return to the Workplace Shell with Ctrl + Esc, and start another program. You can repeat this process for several programs.

Use Alt + Esc to switch from one program to another. (Hold down the Alt key and press Esc repeatedly to switch between running programs.)

7.3   A Multitasking Practice Lesson

If you want to use multitasking, you must remember a few important items.

Many DOS users are confused when they suddenly cannot access a file or a disk drive, although it was still possible just a moment ago. First they think that a computer crash or something equally serious occurred. However, usually it's only the multitasking principle at work.

For example, start the OS/2 2.1 Command Prompt and insert a diskette you don't need anymore into drive A:. Then type:

```
FORMAT A:
```

The formatting process begins and a chart shows the progress of the operation. The percentage increases, indicating that the diskette is being formatted. Using Alt + Esc, switch to the Workplace Shell and start up the *DOS Full Screen* shell. Then type:

```
DIR A:
```

An error message, which indicates that the drive is currently locked by another process, appears. This is called "device lockout"; you'll encounter this frequently when multitasking.

The opposite occurs when you type the following in the DOS Shell:

```
FORMAT B:
```

In this case, you're formatting two diskettes simultaneously. The START command is new in OS/2 2.1. With this command you can start a program in a separate session. For example, suppose that you want to copy a diskette with XCOPY while another process is being performed. For now, insert a diskette in each drive and type:

```
Start "copy diskette A -> B" XCOPY A: B: /S
```

You will find this item again, in quotation marks, in the *Window List*. It's faster to start the commands without entering anything in the *Window List*.

```
Start "copy diskette A-> B" /N XCOPY A: B: /S
```

The parameter "/N" won't start an extra CMD.EXE (the OS/2 2.1 COMMAND.COM). Instead, the command is simply executed in the background.

This is how you can start all the programs that you still want to use. For example, the following command starts the Norton Commander running in the background:

```
START NC
```

As always, Alt + Esc will then let you switch to this program using the *Windows List*.

7.4   File Swapping

Under OS/2 2.1, file swapping occurs exactly as it does in Windows: Over a temporary storage buffer (*Clipboard*). Two temporary buffers are used to do this (one buffer in WIN-OS/2 and one in OS/2). Under normal circumstances, both of these buffers are set to "public". This setting allows both buffers to operate as one. This enables you to move files that you've cut out of a Windows program into an OS/2 program and vice versa.

Once you launch OS/2, you can go to the *System Setup* folder and start the *WIN-OS/2 Setup* program. Set the *Clipboard* switch *Public (share with WIN/OS2)* to on or off. Usually, regardless of which application you're running, you can mark parts of a document and copy them to the temporary storage buffer by using *Edit/Copy*.

With *Edit/Paste*, you can insert the contents of the temporary buffer into another application. You can view the contents of a temporary buffer by selecting Clipboard Viewer from the *Productivity* folder.

DDE

Even under OS/2, Windows' famous Dynamic Data Exchange (DDE) still works. For example, with DDE you can take a table from a spreadsheet and place it in a text document. Any changes you've made in the original spreadsheet immediately appear in the text document's spreadsheet.

NOTE

> To use DDE, don't disable *DOS Background Execution*. Also, set the *Dynamic Data Exchange* switch *Public (share with WIN/OS2)* to ON in the *WIN-OS/2 Setup* program located in the *System Setup* folder.

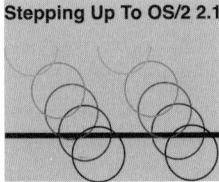

Chapter 8

—— System Setup ——

The utility programs that can configure OS/2 2.1 to your requirements are located in the *System Setup* folder. This is similar to the Window's Control Panel. See Chapter 1 for information on the *Selective Install, Device Driver Install* and *Migrate Applications* programs.

OS/2 2.1 System Setup

8.1   Mouse

Use *Mouse* to configure your mouse.

Under the mouse settings you can use the page labeled *Timing,* for the following:

• Set the double-click speed (at what point two single clicks are considered one double-click).

• Set the *Tracking speed* of the mouse pointer.

To swap the functions of the mouse buttons, use *Setup*. This is helpful to left-handed users.

Under *Mappings*, you can determine which mouse actions will perform which functions. The default settings specify that you move objects with the right mouse button (*Button 2*), you open the pop-up menus by clicking on them once with the right mouse button, and you change the name of an object by holding down Alt and clicking the left mouse button.

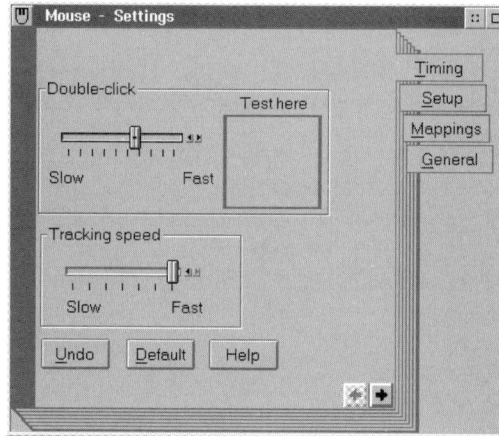

OS/2 2.1 Mouse Settings

8.2   Sound

On the page titled *Warning Beep*, determine whether an additional warning tone (beep) should sound when you make an error. The *General* page contains the general settings.

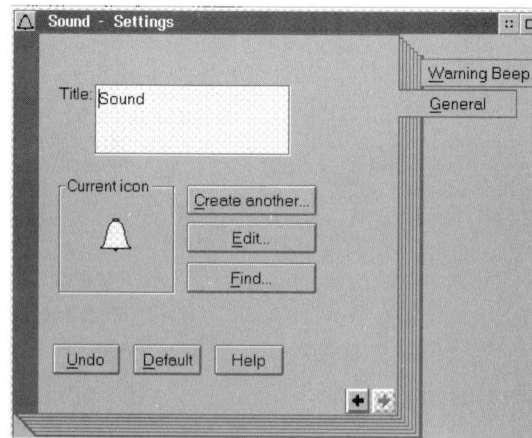

OS/2 2.1 Sound Settings

8.3   System

This is where you set the basic parameters for your system.

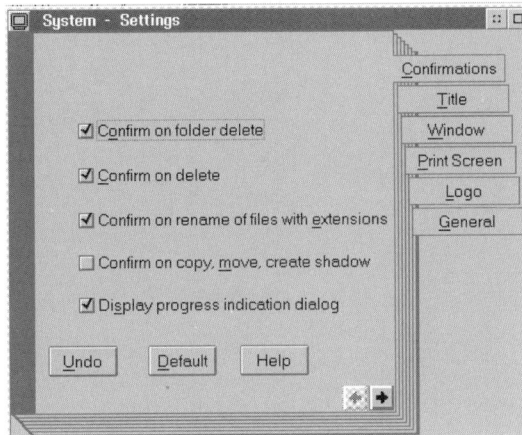

System Confirmations Settings

On the page titled *Confirmations*, you can disable options to switch off several confirmation messages that frequently appear.

Confirm on folder delete
> A confirmation message appears whenever you want to delete a folder.

Confirm on delete
> A confirmation message appears whenever you want to delete a file.

Confirm on rename of files with extensions
> A confirmation message appears whenever you want to rename a file with an extension.

Confirm on copy, move, create shadow
> A confirmation message appears whenever you want to copy, move or create a shadow of a file.

Display progress indication dialog
> A dialog box is displayed that lets you control the progress of the operation.

On the *Title* page, you can decide how the title clashes will be handled under OS/2 2.1.

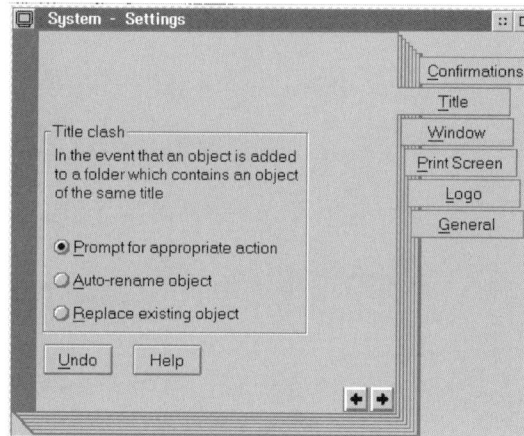

System Settings for object titles

You can select *Prompt for appropriate action, Auto-rename object,* or *Replace existing object*.

On the *Window* page, you can decide how the windows will operate under OS/2 2.1.

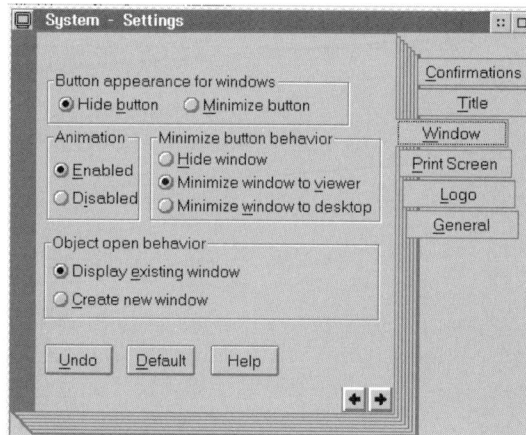

System Window Settings

Set the following under *Button appearance for windows* only for folders, palettes, and drive windows:

> *Minimize button*
>   When you minimize selected objects, they
>   appear as symbols on the Desktop or in the
>   "Minimized Windows Viewer".

> *Hide button*   When you minimize objects, they appear only on the "Windows List". (Click with both mouse buttons on the Desktop simultaneously.)

Under the heading, *Minimize button behavior*, determine what happens to minimized windows.

> *Hide window*
> The window appears only in the "Windows List". (Click both mouse buttons on the Desktop simultaneously.)
>
> *Minimize window in viewer*
> The window appears as an icon in the "Minimized Windows Viewer".
>
> *Minimize window to Desktop*
> The window appears as an icon on the Desktop.

Under *Object open behavior*, you can decide whether to display a window that already exists (*Display existing window*) or whether to create a new window (*Create new window*).

Suppose that you've opened a DOS window and are clicking again on the original icon. In the first example above, you activate the existing window, and in the second, you open another DOS window.

You can also switch *Animation* on (*Enabled*) or off (*Disabled*). You can also switch *Print Screen* on (*Enabled*) or off (*Disabled*) on the *Print Screen* page.

To produce a hardcopy, press the Prt Sc key. If nothing happens, you must set (*Enable*) this option on in the *Print Screen* page.

On the page called *Logo*, you can disable the display of program logos, if their programmers followed the proper guidelines.

> *Indefinite*   Logos are displayed until you close the logo window.
>
> *None*   No logos are displayed.
>
> *Timed*   Logos are displayed for a set time.

On the page called *General*, set the Title and the icon that the object uses.

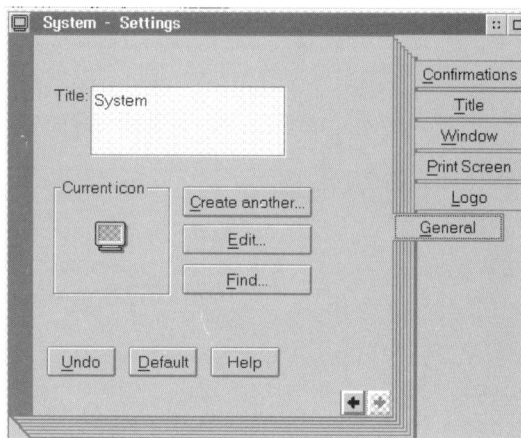

System General Settings

The (Edit) button calls the Icon Editor, which allows you to edit the icon. The (Create Another) button allows you to create a new icon for the object. The (Find) button calls the OS/2 Find program, which lets you search for other objects with icons.

8.4   Country

You can set all the country specific information in Country.

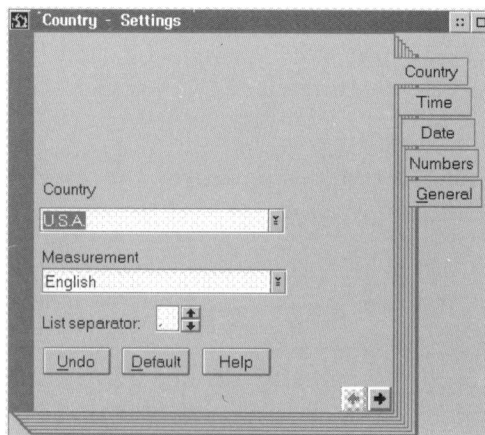

System Country Settings

On the *Country* page, select the country (*USA*), the units of measure (*English*), and the list separator (",").

Under *Time*, you can set the 12 hour format (am, pm), select the 24 hour format and specify the separator. Under *Date*, you can select the correct date format (Month-Day-Year, Day-Month-Year or Year-Month-Day). As a dividing symbol, use the dash, slash, an X or the period.

Under *Numbers*, set the desired currency and number format. The symbol that divides thousands is the comma. Select the dollar sign ($) as the currency symbol. Disable the *Intervening space* and *Leading zero* options.

8.5   Font Palette

Font Palette displays the available fonts. You can change the font of an object by simply selecting a font by clicking on it with the right mouse button and then dragging the font over to the object. If you hold down the Alt key, this change will apply to your entire system. Otherwise, it applies only to the current object.

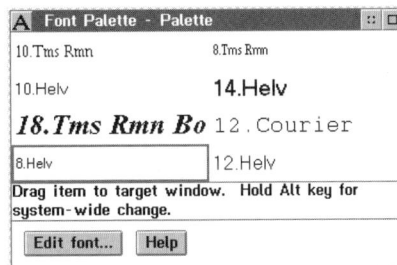

Font Palette

NOTE

For example, drag one of the smaller fonts from the font list to the text under the fonts or to the window title.

With the Edit font... button you can modify the fonts that are displayed in the font list.

8.6   Colors

Use *Color palette* and *Scheme Palette* to modify OS/2 2.1 according to your color preferences.

Color Palette

This provides a palette that contains various colors. Press the right mouse button and simply drag any one of these colors over an

object to change its color to what you selected. If you also hold
down the [Alt] key, the change will apply to the entire system.

For example, to make the Desktop green, simply drag your
favorite shade of green over the Desktop.

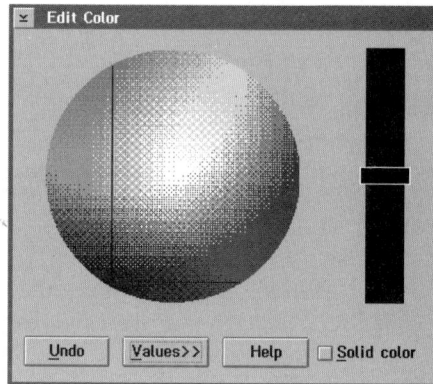

OS/2 2.1 Color Ball

[Edit color...] opens a window in which you can edit colors. You can set
the RGB values (Red-Green-Blue) with the [Values > >] button or you
can change to the HSV setting (Hue-Saturation-Value).

The *Solid color* option prevents dithering. It's very difficult to
read some fonts on dithered backgrounds, for example.

Use the mouse and the crosshairs in the big color wheel to
preselect colors for your final selection.

Scheme Palette

With *Scheme Palette*, you can easily color the sides of the window
borders.

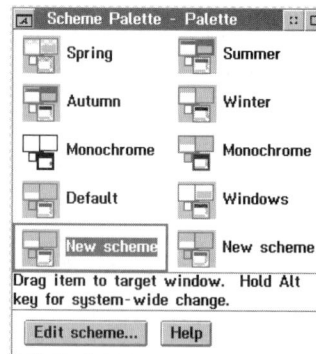

Scheme   Palette

The window already contains eight prepared color combinations that you can easily drag over the Desktop (while holding down the [Alt] key). If you drag a scheme over an open window, only this window reflects the changes.

With the [Edit scheme...] button, you can also create your own color scheme.

In the *Window area* list, or on the left side using the right mouse button, select the element that you want to color. Then you can adjust the colors in the *Color Palette* as described. Finally, under *Border width*, you can adjust the width of the window borders.

8.7   Spooler

Clicking on *Spooler* displays the *Spooler Settings* notebook. On its single page, called *Spool Path*, you can enter a new path.

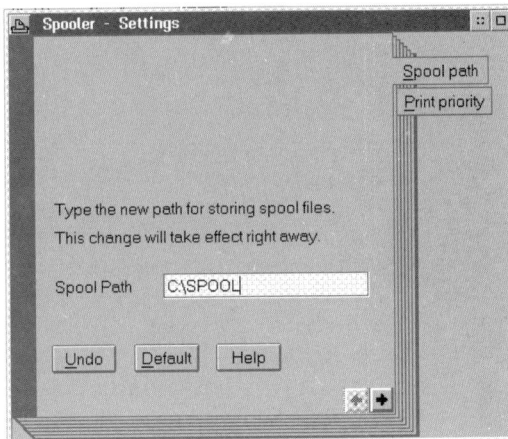

Spooler   -   Settings

If you print a lot each day, you can move the path to an extra disk drive, so you can free the system drive.

Enable or disable the spooler in the *Spooler* Object menu.

8.8   Keyboard

This section allows you to adjust the keyboard settings according to your requirements.

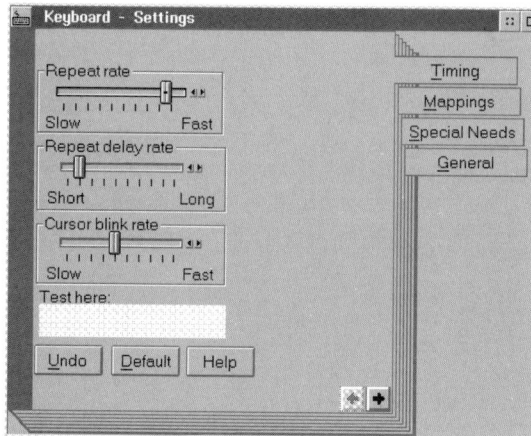

Keyboard - Settings

Keyboard timings

On the page labeled *Timing*, you can set the speed of the clock rates:

Repeat rate	This setting determines how fast characters will repeat when you press a key.
Repeat delay rate	This value specifies how long a key must be pressed before the repeat function is enabled.
Cursor blink rate	This setting determines how quickly a cursor blinks.

On the page titled *Mappings*, you can decide which keyboard commands should open the Object menu (*Displaying pop-up menus*) and what key you press to edit a title text (*Editing title text*).

The *Special Needs* page provides several other possibilities for adjusting special keyboard settings, such as the *Keyboard Response* and the *Settings time-out*.

Acceptance delay defines the amount of time a key must be pressed before that keystroke is read. You can also set the *Repeat rate* and the *Delay until repeat*.

All these values are active only when the *Settings activation* is switched to *On*. Then you can enter a *Setting time-out*, after which this setting may be deactivated again.

8.9   System Clock

When you double-click *System Clock*, a clock is displayed on the screen.

OS/2 2.1 Clock

To change the clock's appearance, use *Open/Settings* from the *Object* menu. To modify the clock display, open the *View* page in the *System Clock Settings* notebook.

Under *Information*, you can determine what will be displayed: only the time (*Time only*), only the date (*Date only*), or both (*Both date and time*). Under *Mode*, select either analog or digital display.

Disable the *Show title bar* option to hide the clock's title. However, when you do this, you won't be able to move the clock.

Setting the alarm

The *Alarm* page sets the Alarm options. Enable *Audio alarm*, if you want only an alarm to sound. To display a message window on the screen, activate *Message Box*.

Setting the system date and clock time

Type either:

DATE

or:

```
TIME
```

on OS/2's command line to assign a date and time. You can also set the time and date on the page marked *Date/Time*. Here you can easily set the system date and system time with your mouse.

8.10 WIN-OS/2 Setup

These settings determine how Windows and OS/2 exchange data.

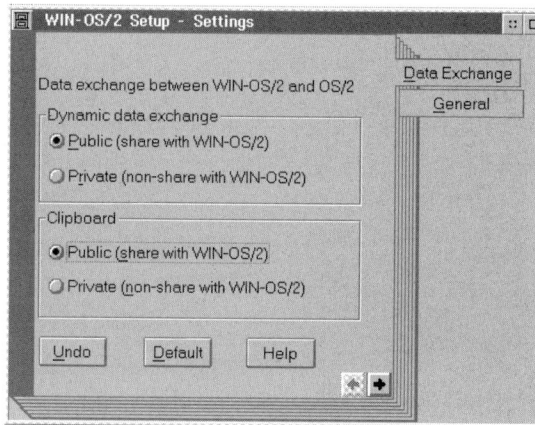

WIN-OS/2 2.1 Setup

Dynamic Data Exchange

This switch allows Windows to share DDE information with other public Windows and OS/2 sessions. It can be set to *Public (share with WIN-OS/2)* or *Private (non-share with WIN-OS/2)*.

Clipboard

This switch allows Windows to share Clipboard information with other public Windows and OS/2 sessions. It can be set to *Public (share with WIN-OS/2)* or *Private (non-share with WIN-OS/2)*.

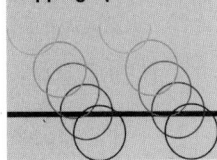

Chapter 9

Printing Under OS/2 2.1

Printing under OS/2 2.1 is similar to printing under DOS or Windows applications.

Whenever you print something under OS/2, nothing seems to happen at first. The Print Manager intercepts the print output and temporarily stores the data either on the hard drive, in the queue or the spooler.

OS/2 checks whether the printer is ready. If so, the data is sent in small portions from the spooler to the printer until printing is completed.

While this is happening, you can continue to run another application and send a completely different job to the printer. The Print Manager intercepts this job and temporarily stores it in the spooler. Then the Print Manager waits to perform the actual printing until the previous job is complete.

OS/2 2.1 even has the power to manage spooled printers. To the user, it seems that only one printer is available, although, for example, three printers may be set up. As soon as a print job is sent, the Print Manager finds the first available printer, or the printer with the lightest load, and sends the job to its spooler.

To print a file, select the object and then the *Print* item in the *Object* menu. You can also drag the symbol of a text file over the printer icon. After a short wait, the print job is performed.

9.1 Printer Installation

Installing the printer involves telling the OS/2 2.1 operating system that a printer exists, where and how it's connected, and how to make it work. OS/2 needs this information to function properly.

Usually the printer is installed during the OS/2 2.1 installation. However, sometimes a printer is installed after the system is installed (e.g., if you buy a new printer).

To install a new printer driver, select the *Object* menu of a current printer driver and select *Create another*. Enter a *New name* for the printer and then select the [Create] button in the *Create another* window. Click the [Install new printer driver] button in the window labeled *Create a Printer*.

You'll see the *Install New Printer Driver* window. The window displays a list containing all the available printers. Select the matching driver and click on [Install] to copy the appropriate printer driver files to your hard drive.

Insert the diskette containing the OS/2 printer drivers (Printer Driver 1-5) in drive A: and click on [Refresh]. If this diskette doesn't contain your printer driver, insert another one and click on [Refresh] again. Exit the *Install New Printer Driver* window.

Now select the correct printer driver in the *Create a Printer* window and click on [Create]. A new symbol appears on your Desktop representing the printer you just installed.

9.2   Spooler

The spooler is a tool similar to a disk cache. It helps make a fast computer less dependent on slow peripherals.

All the data waiting to be printed is temporarily stored in the spooler. Your computer ignores your printer until it's ready to accept the print job. Then the computer sends data in small portions to the printer.

The spooler is simply a file that temporarily contains all the data that's sent to it. As a result, few settings are required on a spooler.

To determine where this file should be located, open the *System Setup*. You'll find the *System Setup* in the *OS/2 System* folder.

Double-click on *Spooler* to display the *Spooler Settings* notebook. On its one page, called *Spool Path*, enter a new path for your spooler file. If there is a lot of output, you can store the path on a separate drive so you can free the system drive.

On the *Spooler* Object menu you can enable or disable the spooler.

9.3   Printing from DOS Windows and Windows

You can print from your DOS applications as you always have.

In the DOS settings under PRINT_TIMEOUT, you can also assign a time-out, in seconds, that a DOS application can let pass until it prints. From that point, OS/2 considers the print job finished and passes it along to the Print Manager.

Printing with Windows

You can also print under Windows as normal. However, when you install a printer driver under Windows, make certain to assign LPTn.OS2 as the printer port; otherwise conflicts could occur.

9.4   Making Hardcopies

A hardcopy is simply a printout of the screen. To produce a hardcopy, press the (Prt Sc) (Print Screen) key.

If there is no response, activate the *Print Screen* option in the *System* notebook (under *System Setup* in the *OS/2 System*).

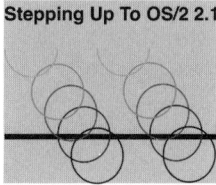

Chapter 10

Productivity Folder

The *Productivity* folder contains many useful utility programs, including the PM Diary, the *Enhanced Editor*, the *Icon Editor*, *PM Chart*, *PM Terminal*, *Pulse*, and *Seek and Scan Files*.

10.1 PM Diary

The PM Diary consists of fourteen programs that work with each other. It contains everything you need to perform your daily tasks.

The following programs make up the PM Diary:

Name	Purpose
Activities List	Creates a list from the Daily Planner
Alarms	For setting the alarm times
Calculator	A small pocket calculator
Calendar	Months/Years Calendar
Daily Planner	Daily planner
Database	A small database/card index
Monthly Planner	Monthly planner
Notepad	Note pad
Planner Archive	Archive for calendar entries
Spreadsheet	A small spreadsheet
Sticky Pad	Small "Post-It" notes for the screen
To Do List	A list of jobs and activities
To Do List Archive	Archive for the To Do List
Tune Editor	Editor for alarm tunes

The following are brief descriptions of the individual programs.

Activities List

This section displays a list of your activities. These activities are taken from the information in the *Daily Planner*.

To display a specific activity in the *Daily Planner*, double-click on it.

Alarms

This program is the heart of the PM Diary. Here you enter the important appointment times and set an alarm that will sound at these times.

The window displays all the alarm times that are active at any time.

Setting the alarm

Under *Alarms/Set alarm...*, enter any new appointment times. Set the status to *On* and select a *Number* that hasn't been used yet. In the settings, you can decide whether the alarm should sound *Every Day*, only on *Weekdays*, or on specific days. Now enter the clock time for the alarm.

Under *Graphic*, you can select a graphic that will be displayed on the screen when the alarm goes off. Under *Comment*, you can enter an appropriate reminder or message.

Determine how the alarm should appear under *Action*:

Activate first Alarm time occurrence only.
        The alarm sounds only for the first entry.

Activate every Alarm time occurrence.
        The alarm sounds for every entry.

Pop Up (If not set, Alarm sounds once only.)
        A window appears. Only an auditory alarm will go off if this option isn't activated.

Execute comment as command at Alarm time.
        When the alarm sounds, the line entered under *Comment* acts as a command line and is passed to the OS/2 Shell.

The *Customize* menu lets you set several options. Enter your default planning file under *Customize/Set master planner file*. Under *Customize/Sound limit*, set the duration of the alarm tone.

When the alarm sounds, switch it off temporarily by activating *Snooze*. Under *Customize/Snooze period* you can determine when the alarm should sound again. You can also cancel the snooze feature with *Alarms/Cancel snooze*.

Up to ten alarm times can be active at a time.

Calculator

This is a small pocket calculator with a line printer.

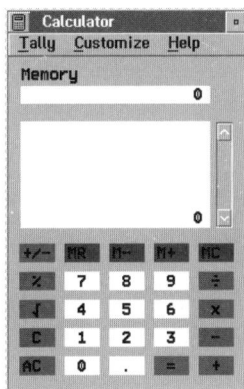

Calculator

You can use this *Calculator* like you use a normal calculator. Click on the keys with the mouse or use the keyboard.

Clear the electronic roll of paper with *Tally/Clear tally roll* or print it with *Tally/Print*.

The *Customize/Floating point* setting provides a scientific calculator with floating point arithmetic. You can select the *Customize/Fixed* option if you want to use a calculator with two decimal places.

Customize/Num Lock allows you to use the mouse to switch your Num Lock key on or off.

Calendar

The *Calendar* provides an overview of several years.

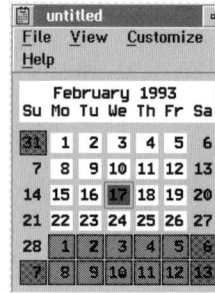

Calendar

To display the next year or the previous year, use *View/Next year* and *View/Previous year*. At this point, you can also switch over to the *Daily Planner* with a double-click.

Use *File/Refresh current file* to re-enter any dates you may have changed. Use the *File/Statistics for current year* command to create a statistical overview of your activities.

Daily Planner

The *Daily Planner* is similar to a pocket calendar. You can enter all your daily appointments here.

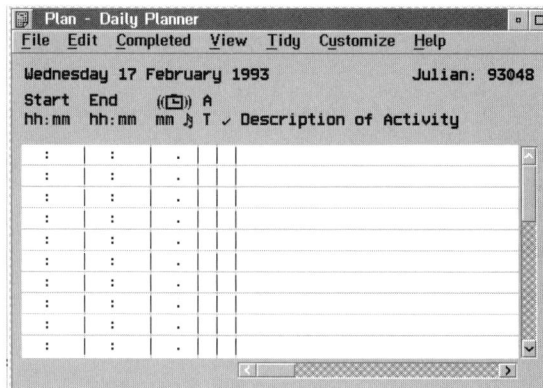

Daily Planner

Enter the appointment's beginning and ending times. You can also enter, in minutes, how long before the actual appointment the alarm should sound. Enter a comment that explains why you set the alarm.

Database

The *Database* is a small electronic card index. This can be used to create a telephone directory, for example.

Select *File/New* to enter a name in your database. To enter a new set of data, select *Edit/Add a new record*. Now fill in the eight fields with the appropriate information and store it with *File/Save*. Continue this process until you've entered all the information. Then exit the entry mode with *Edit/Cancel edit*.

A little cursor blinks in a small field labeled *Search Key*. To find an entry, type the first few letters in the name.

Under *View/Line 1..8*, you can assign a line that will act as an index field.

Monthly Planner

The *Monthly Planner* provides an overview of the entire month.

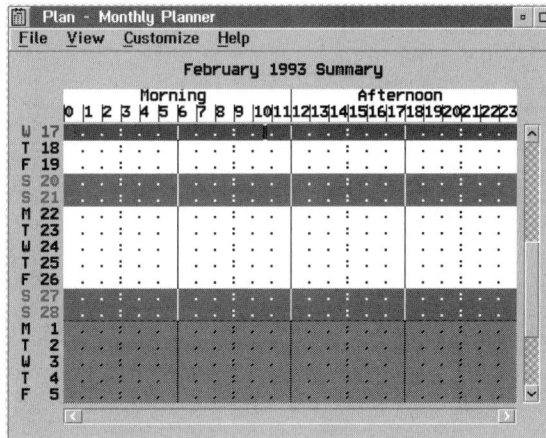

Monthly Planner

Select the appropriate month with *View/Month*. To see the subsequent or previous month, select *View/Next month* or *View/Previous month*.

Double-clicking on a specific day will open the *Daily Planner* with the appropriate settings.

Note Pad

This is a small electronic notepad that contains five pages (each page can contain up to 180 characters).

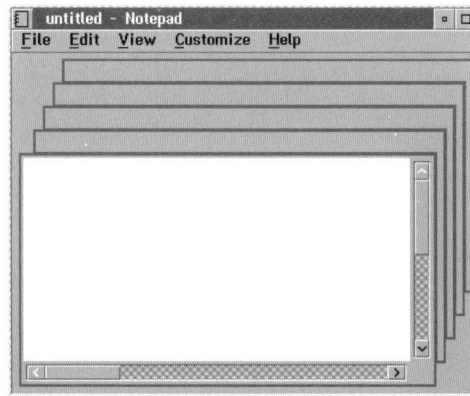

Notepad

The top line of each page is always visible so you can enter a title. To activate a specific page, simply click on the page title.

Planner Archive

All the dates on the daily planner are archived in the *Planner Archive*. Enter the list of activities here and sort it according to various criteria (*View/Sort...*).

You can also set up a list of statistics (*File/Statistics...*).

Spreadsheet

OS/2 2.1 even includes a small spreadsheet. This *Spreadsheet* has a page consisting of 25 columns and 80 rows. These cell addresses are A1 to Z80.

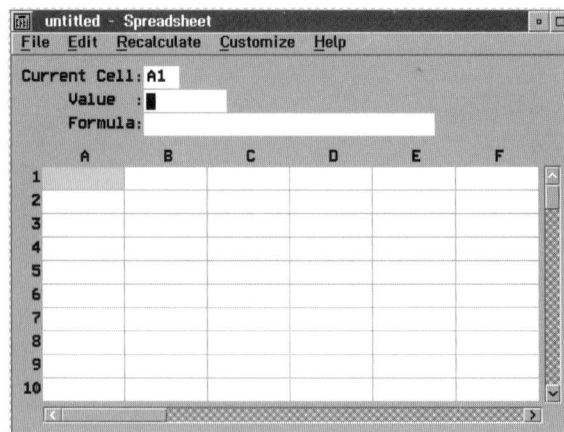

Spreadsheet

You can enter numbers, text, or formulas in each cell. To enter a number or text, move to the corresponding field and type the number or text.

Click on the field labeled *Formula* to enter a formula. A formula contains calculating instructions made up of cell names (A1, B5,...) and the corresponding operations. You can use the following operations:

+ Addition

- Subtraction

* Multiplication

/ Division

[] Brackets

You must use brackets because spreadsheets don't perform multiplication before other operations. For example:

```
2 + 4 * 5
```

produces 30 instead of 22. So, you must place brackets around the numbers to be multiplied to obtain the correct result of 22:

```
2 + [ 4 * 5 ]
```

You can use the sum check to calculate a field:

```
@ Sum
```

For example:

```
A1@B2
```

is the same as:

```
A1+A2+B1+B2
```

Under *Recalculate* you can determine how a spreadsheet should be recalculated. Normally, the spreadsheet is automatically recalculated when you enter a new value.

Sticky Pad

The *Sticky Pad* is an electronic version of the famous Post-It® note pads. You can stick these small notes to the windows on your Desktop.

Once you've started the *Sticky Pad*, write a message on the yellow pad.

Now open the window where you want to place the note and drag the yellow pad into it. The window is activated. The note stays in the foreground. To anchor the note on the bottom window border, minimize it to an icon.

To read the note, double-click on it.

To Do list

Enter your daily tasks in the *To Do List*. Assign each one a priority (*View/Sort...*) and the list will sort your tasks according to priority.

To mark the tasks you've completed, use *Mark current item as completed*.

To Do List Archive

All the activities in the *To Do List* are archived in the *To Do List Archive*. You can examine this list and sort its contents according to various criteria (*View/Sort...*).

Tune Editor

Use the *Tune Editor* to change the alarm melodies. Change the individual settings (*Note*, *Pitch*, *Value*) with the sliding scales.

10.2   Icon Editor

With the *Icon Editor*, you can create or modify icons (symbols such as the *Shredder*), pointers (such as the mouse pointer), or simple bitmaps (pictures such as the OS/2 startup screen logo).

Using the Icon Editor

To create an icon, first open the *File* menu and click on *New*. A window, in which you must choose what you want to draw, appears. To make your selection, click on *Icon*, *Pointer*, or *Bitmap*, and then on OK. If you want to create a bitmap, you must also determine its size in pixels.

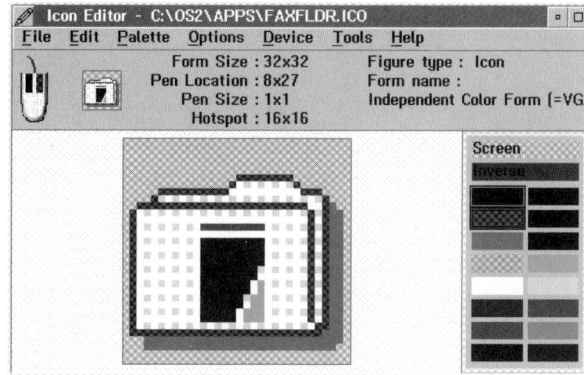

Icon Editor

A window appears which has a drawing surface in the middle. The right border contains all the available colors.

Individual elements

The top two colors are important because they are "logical" colors. The color labeled *Screen* shows the current background color (light green). This is similar to a small piece of glass. The violet color, labeled *Inverse*, is a variation of this. The parts of the screen that are filled with this color will later invert the colors underneath them (the *Screen* color).

You can use the remaining colors to color various elements in your drawing. They will appear later as they do here and will cover any color under them.

To draw with any color, click on it with the left or the right mouse button. In this way, you can also draw with two colors.

To remove the current color combination, use the mouse in the upper-left corner. The left and right mouse buttons have the corresponding colors. To the right of this mouse is a small area in which you can preview the drawing in its original size.

When you draw, move the mouse over the drawing surface as you press the left or right mouse button, as you would do in other drawing programs.

There is no eraser for icons and pointers. If you make a mistake, simply draw over them with the color *Screen* or the current background color. You can also double-click on the spot to be erased with the brush (the little square that you move with your mouse).

To cancel all the recent changes, use the *Edit /Undo* command or press Alt + Backspace.

Save the completed drawing with *File/Save as...*. Enter a filename in the window that appears. If a file with the same name already exists, a confirmation message appears. Click on *Save* to actually save the file on the hard drive.

Symbols (icons) are assigned the *.ICO extension. Pointers are assigned the *.PTR extension. Bitmaps are assigned the *.BTM extension.

File/Save will later save any changes made to an existing drawing, under the same name.

Block operations

Use the *Edit/Select all* command to mark the entire picture, on which you're working, as a block. *Edit/Select* provides a new mouse pointer that enables you to use a rubber band (e.g., as under GEM or in the Workplace Shell). The entire picture is then defined as a block. Then you can work on entire blocks. You can copy, cut, color, or flip them on their horizontal or vertical axis.

Edit/Copy helps you copy a marked block to the temporary storage buffer (*Clipboard*). From there, you can insert a block into another picture or even into another application. Unlike *Edit/Copy*, *Edit/Cut* cuts out a portion of the picture and stores this clipping in the storage buffer.

With *Edit/Paste* you can move a clipping from the *Clipboard* to a picture you're working on. A frame then appears on your picture. You can grab this frame and move it out of the way. Use *Edit/Clear* to erase a marked block.

Edit/Stretch Paste enables you to move a clipping from the buffer and insert it into a clipping that was previously marked. Frequently, some of the forms are lost because of scaling.

You can mirror blocks horizontally or vertically by marking a block and then using the *Edit/Flip horizontal* and *Edit/Flip vertical* options.

It's also possible to draw circles with the blocks. Mark a block as before and select *Edit/Circle* to obtain a circle that fits exactly into the block and is filled with the color of the left mouse button.

Options

The *Option* menu contains several functions that are used for drawing. Activate the options by clicking on them once; a check mark will appear in the menu. Clicking the option again deactivates it.

Clicking on *Options/Test* when you enter the drawing surface causes the mouse pointer to change into the picture you're working on. This lets you experiment with different mouse pointers.

The *Grid* option places a grid over a picture. This enables you to see the individual points of the image.

With *Options/X Background*, all points on an image that have the screen color *Screen* or its inverse (*Inverse*) color will be crossed out with x's.

Options/Draw straight helps you draw straight lines. You can then draw only in the directions in which you've moved the mouse.

Modify the brush you're using by selecting *Options/Pen size*. Brush sizes from 1x1 to 9x9 pixels are provided. It's easier to do this by entering the desired dot size as [Ctrl] + n. For "n", press one of the numbers to obtain a square brush in that size.

For a rectangular brush, mark a block with the appropriate size with *Edit/Select* and then select the *Options/Set pen shape* command.

Options/Preferences provides another menu with the following settings:

Safe Prompting
> This default option causes a confirmation message to appear when you exit the Icon Editor after changing a picture.

Suppress Warnings
> Use this option to switch off the confirmation messages from the Icon Editor. However, doing this can be dangerous.

Save State on exit
> If you enable this option, all the settings you've made will be saved. The next time you start your computer, your work environment will be changed accordingly.

Display status area
> Use this option to eliminate the gray highlighted area above a picture and below a menu. This produces a larger drawing surface.

Reset options and modes
> This command returns all options to the default settings.

Mouse and other types of pointers must have a point that's programmed to execute a command. This point is called the "hotspot" and is usually the very tip of the pointer.

Use the *Options/Hotspot* command to define the hotspots you create under OS/2. To set the new hotspot in the desired location, use the crosshairs and click the left mouse button.

Changing colors

You can also mix your own colors. Click on the color you want to change with the left mouse button to enable the *Edit* command from the *Palette* menu.

A window, containing slide rules that can be used to mix the hue from the *RGB* (Red-Green-Blue) colors, appears. You can also enter the values directly. Lower values signify colors with lower intensities.

It's also possible to set the *HSV* (Hue-Saturation-Value) mode. Determine the hue on the upper slide, the saturation (from gray to full color saturation) in the middle, and the value on the bottom slide.

Use the *Palette/Swap colors* to swap the two colors of the left and right mouse buttons. With *Preserve figure*, the current drawing won't be affected and with *Don't preserve figure*, the two corresponding colors will also be swapped inside the current drawing.

Once you've created an attractive color palette, you can save it with *Palette/Save as...* so you can load it later with *Palette/Open*. You can always restore the default settings with *Palette/Load default palette*.

Additional functions

Two additional tools are located in the *Tools* menu. These are a color fill tool and a tool to search for a specific color in a picture.

To fill a closed area with a color, use the *Tools/Color fill* command. Be sure that the surrounding line actually is closed; otherwise, the color "leaks out" of the area you want filled. (You can repair the damage with *Edit/Undo*.)

After activating the *Tools/Find color* command, the mouse pointer changes to a question mark. Use the point of the arrow to click on a color in the picture you're working on. This changes the left or the right mouse button to the corresponding color.

Creating a new icon

To create new icons for your programs, first you must activate the *Icon Editor*. To do this, open the Object menu of the appropriate icon and click on *Open/Settings*. Now click on *General*. Beside *Current icon* (you'll see the [Edit...] button. Click on this to modify the desired icon. Once you've done this, save the icon with *File/Save*.

Any icons you may have created earlier should have been copied to the temporary file already. Now, you can insert them with *Edit/Paste*.

10.3 OS/2 System Editor

The *OS/2 System Editor* is a very simple ASCII editor. You can use this editor to modify the CONFIG.SYS, the AUTOEXEC.BAT, and *.BAT or *.CMD files.

Under *File/New*, delete the current contents of the Editor window. If you haven't saved any changes yet, a confirmation message appears. If you don't want to save these changes, click on [Discard].

In the *File/Open* window, you can load a file into the Editor.

```
/ OS/2 System Editor - C:\CONFIG.BAK                          □ |□|
 File  Edit  Options  Help
IFS=C:\OS2\HPFS.IFS   /CACHE:64 /CRECL:4 /AUTOCHECK:C
PROTSHELL=C:\OS2\PMSHELL.EXE
SET USER_INI=C:\OS2\OS2.INI
SET SYSTEM_INI=C:\OS2\OS2SYS.INI
SET OS2_SHELL=C:\OS2\CMD.EXE
SET AUTOSTART=PROGRAMS,TASKLIST,FOLDERS,CONNECTIONS
SET RUNWORKPLACE=C:\OS2\PMSHELL.EXE
SET COMSPEC=C:\OS2\CMD.EXE
LIBPATH=.;C:\OS2\DLL;C:\OS2\MDOS;C:\;C:\OS2\APPS\DLL;
SET
PATH=C:\OS2;C:\OS2\SYSTEM;C:\OS2\MDOS\WINOS2;C:\OS2\INSTALL;C:\;C:\OS2\MDOS;C:\
OS2\APPS;
SET
DPATH=C:\OS2;C:\OS2\SYSTEM;C:\OS2\MDOS\WINOS2;C:\OS2\INSTALL;C:\;C:\OS2\BITMAP;
C:\OS2\MDOS;C:\OS2\APPS;
SET PROMPT=$i[$p]
SET HELP=C:\OS2\HELP;C:\OS2\HELP\TUTORIAL;
SET GLOSSARY=C:\OS2\HELP\GLOSS;
SET IPF_KEYS=SBCS
PRIORITY_DISK_IO=YES
FILES=20
DEVICE=C:\OS2\TESTCFG.SYS
DEVICE=C:\OS2\DOS.SYS
DEVICE=C:\OS2\PMDD.SYS
BUFFERS=30
IOPL=YES
DISKCACHE=256,LW
```

System Editor

Options/Word wrap determines whether text should break at the end of a line (*On*) or the text lines should be displayed in their actual full length (*Off*).

Save your completed modifications with *File/Save* or with *File/Save as...* if you want to rename the file.

Under *File/Autosave...*, you can specify the number of changes that must occur before a file is saved automatically by enabling *Autosave on* in the displayed window.

To cancel a change you've just made, press [Alt] + [Backspace] or select the *Edit/Undo typing* command.

Block operations

As in almost all the other programs, you can also work with blocks in the *System Editor*.

To mark a block, place the mouse pointer at the beginning of the block and press the left mouse button while dragging the mouse to the end of the block. Then release the mouse button.

The *Edit/Select all* command marks the entire block of text as a single unit. To delete a block marked in this way, press [Del] or select the *Edit/Clear* command.

Use *Edit/Copy* to copy the block into the *Clipboard* and *Edit/Cut* to delete the block.

Any text already in the *Clipboard* can be inserted into the text at the cursor position with *Edit/Paste*.

Search and Replace

Open the *Find* window with the *Edit/Find* command or ⌨Ctrl⌨ + ⌨F⌨. Enter a text that you want to find. If you want the Editor to ignore upper and lowercase characters, first switch off the *Case sensitive* option.

When the *Wrap* option is activated, the entire text is searched. When this option isn't activated, the text is searched only from the current cursor position to the end.

Any text that is found will appear in the window as a marked text. If nothing appears in this window, the found text may be hidden behind the *Find* window. In this case, move the window so you can see the text.

To delete the found text in the original, click on one of the ⌷Change⌷ buttons. Using *Change to*, you can enter a text to replace the found text.

Once you've inserted a replacement text, you can select several options:

⌷Change, then find⌷	Each time you activate this option, you swap the found text, then the program continues to search and pause.
	Click on *Find* if you don't want to replace the text or click on ⌷Change, then find⌷ to replace the text and then resume the search.
⌷Change⌷	Replaces the text.
⌷Change all⌷	Replaces the search text with the replacement text in the entire document. With *Wrap* disabled, the program searches only from the current location to the end of the document.

Under *Options*, you can select the font and color. *Options/Select font...* opens a window for setting a font (*Name*), pitch (*Size*), and style (*Style*).

You can also determine whether the text should be outlined (*Outline*), underlined (*Underline*), or crossed out (*Strikeout*).

The *Sample* list displays a sample text in the selected font.

Use (Apply) to display an example of the text in the selected font. The window disappears and the settings are activated only after (OK) is clicked.

Color

Assign the color of the text displayed on the screen under *Options/Set colors*. Then select a color for the text (*Foreground*) and a color for the background (*Background*).

Use (Apply) to display an example of the text in the selected colors in the Editor. When (OK) is clicked, the *Set colors* window disappears and the settings are activated.

10.4 Enhanced Editor

The *Enhanced Editor* is the "big brother" of the *OS/2 System Editor*. In this editor, you can work on large documents and even use several windows simultaneously.

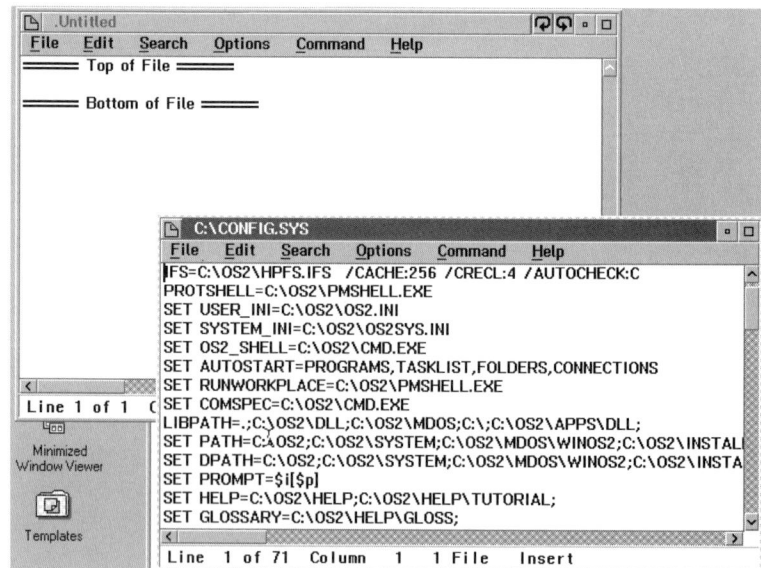

Enhanced Editor

When you start the *Enhanced Editor* without any set parameters, at first you see a blank page, a blinking cursor, a *Top of File* above, and a *Bottom of File* below.

Although you can use this editor for entering text, the *Enhanced Editor* is capable of much more. For example, you can work on more than one file at a time and create keyboard macros.

Using the Enhanced Editor

To delete the current file in the Editor, use *File/New*. A confirmation message appears if this file hasn't been saved yet. *File/Open, Untitled* opens a new, empty Editor window. *File/Quit* closes the current file without saving it.

To load a file into the Editor, use *File/Open....* *File/Import text file...* inserts a text file into the current text.

File/Add will add another file to the chain or ring of files in the current Editor window. *Ring enabled* must be set active in the *Options/Preferences* submenu. Set *Rotate buttons* active in the *Options/Frame* control submenu to move through the file chain.

Save a file with *File/Save as...* and assign it a filename. *File/Save* then always saves the file under the current name.

Use *File/Print file...* to print the current document.

Block operations

To mark blocks in this editor, use the familiar CUA method (as under Windows) or the expanded, easy-to-use marking mode of the *Enhanced Editor*.

Switch between these two modes by using *Options/Preferences...* and *Advanced marking*. When this option isn't active, mark text as you do under Windows.

Use the mouse to mark a block by placing the mouse cursor at the beginning of the block, holding down the left mouse button, and dragging the mouse to the end of the block. Then release the mouse.

Additional features

Select *Edit/Unmark*, the key combination [Alt] + [U] or double-click somewhere in the text to delete all markings.

To mark a single character, press [Alt] + [Z]. You can expand a mark by pressing [Alt]+ [Z] again a little farther down and to the right of the original location.

Use [Alt] + [L] to mark an entire line. You can expand a mark by pressing [Alt] + [L] again a little farther down and to the right of the original location.

With Alt + B, you can mark the upper-left corner of a block. A little farther down you can mark the lower-right corner with Alt + B.

Use *Edit/Copy* to copy the block out of the temporary storage buffer and use *Edit/Cut* to delete the block.

To insert text that's located in the temporary file into the text at the current cursor location, use *Edit/Paste*.

Edit/Paste lines inserts the text a line at a time. At the end of each line in the temporary file, a line break will be inserted in the text. In *Edit/Paste block*, the text being inserted is handled and inserted as one block.

You can do even more with the marked text:

Use *Edit/Copy mark* to copy marked text to the current cursor position. *Edit/Move mark* moves the text to the current cursor position. With *Edit/Overlay mark*, you can copy the marked text over the existing text, starting at the cursor position. *Edit/Adjust mark* fills the empty spot that the marked text formerly occupied with spaces. Use the *Edit/Style...* command to assign any of the various fonts to the marked text.

Search and Replace

The *Search* menu contains commands for searching and replacing text.

Use *Search/Search...* or Ctrl + S to open the *Search* window. Here, you can insert a text that the *Enhanced Editor* should search for in the document. Disable the *Ignore case* option if you want the program to consider upper and lowercase characters.

When the *Reverse search* option is activated, the text is searched from the current cursor position to the beginning of the document. When this option is switched off, the text is searched only from the current cursor position to the end of the document.

To replace all found text passages with the replacement text, activate *Change all occurrences*.

If *Marked area* is active, the search and replace process will occur only in the marked area.

Once a text is found, it appears in a green double circle. If this doesn't occur, the text may be hidden behind the *Search* window. In this case, move the window so you can see the text.

If you click on only one of the [Change] buttons, the found text in the original document is deleted.

Under *Replace*, you can insert a text that will replace the found text. Once you've inserted a replacement text, you have several additional replacement options:

[Find]	Resumes a search
[Change]	Replaces text
[Change, then find]	This replaces text, then resumes the search and pauses again. You can click on [Find] if you don't want to replace the text.
	Click [Change, then find] if you want to replace the text and resume the search.
[Find, cancel]	This searches for text and closes the Search window.

Start a new search with [Ctrl] + [F] or *Search/Find next*. If you've continued your work but want to replace text, press [Ctrl] + [C].

Setting bookmarks

Setting bookmarks is very useful in longer documents. The *Enhanced Editor* is able to work with these bookmarks. Assign names to the bookmarks and store them in the extended attributes. So you can even insert bookmarks into your CONFIG.SYS without affecting its ability to function.

Set the bookmarks with *Search/Bookmarks/Set...* in the *Set Bookmark* window. Enter a name for the bookmark, for example:

```
Proofread again!
```

To store the bookmark in the document permanently, click on *Set permanent*. If you click only *Set*, the bookmark will be lost once you close the Editor window.

NOTE   For a temporary bookmark, use *Set*. To save the bookmark in the extended attributes, use *Set permanent*.

If you've used the *Set permanent* setting, select the menu item *Search/Bookmarks/List...* or press [Ctrl] + [B] to display a list that contains all the bookmarks in that file. Double-clicking on a bookmark places the cursor in the correct location in the text.

You can also jump from one bookmark to another with the menu item *Search/Bookmarks/Next* and *Search/Bookmarks/Previous*.

Default settings

The *Enhanced Editor* contains many settings. To specify these settings, activate *Options/Preferences/Settings...*:

Tabs	Sets the tab spaces for charts.
Margins	Sets the margins. Under *Paragraphs*, enter the number of spaces each paragraph should be indented.
Colors	Sets the colors.
Paths	Here you set the individual paths:
	Autosave path sets the path where *Autosave* temporarily saves the text.
	All temporary files are located under *Temporary path*. Enter a RAM disk if you have one.
Autosave	Indicates the number of changes that must occur before a file is automatically saved.
	Use the *Options/Autosave...* command to display information about the current *Autosave* file.
Fonts	Select the font, in which you want to display the text on the screen.
	You should select *System Monospaced* in size 12x8, without attributes.
Keys	Here you can redefine some keystroke combinations with the (Enter) key and adjust them to your personal requirements.

Options/Messages... displays a list of the last messages the *Enhanced Editor* sent to you.

To adjust the appearance of the *Enhanced Editor* according to your own preferences, enable or disable various options from the *Options/Frame controls* menu.

Status line	Switches the display of the status line on or off.
Message line	When this option is active, a message line is displayed. Otherwise, the messages appear only briefly.
Scrollbars	Switches the scrollbars on or off.
Rotate buttons	Switches the two arrow-ring buttons in the upper-right corner of the title bar on or off. You need these arrow-ring buttons when you've loaded several documents in the Editor window using the *File/Add* menu item or, for instance, from the command line.
Info at top	Status and message lines are displayed in the upper portion of a window when this option is activated.
Prompting	Enable this option to display a small help text on the status or message line for every menu item selection.

With *Options/Save options*, you can permanently save your settings for the *Enhanced Editor* to the hard drive.

Editor commands

Use *Command/Command dialog...* to execute the powerful Editor commands or even OS/2 commands. Clicking on *Command/Command dialog* displays a window. In the upper portion of this window you can choose to repeat the execution of one of the last 25 commands by using the ⬆ and ⬇ cursor keys.

You can place the command on the entry line. For example, if you enter:

```
KEY 78 -
```

A dividing line, consisting of 78 dashes, appears.

The command:

```
DIR C:\ /S
```

opens a new document and inserts the complete directory of your C: partition into it.

After these commands are executed you can switch between these
commands using the cursor keys or with the mouse.

For more information about the Editor commands, refer to the Help
file.

10.5 PM Chart

With *PM Chart* by Micrografx you can create sketches and
diagrams. When you activate *PM Chart*, you'll see a blank
worksheet.

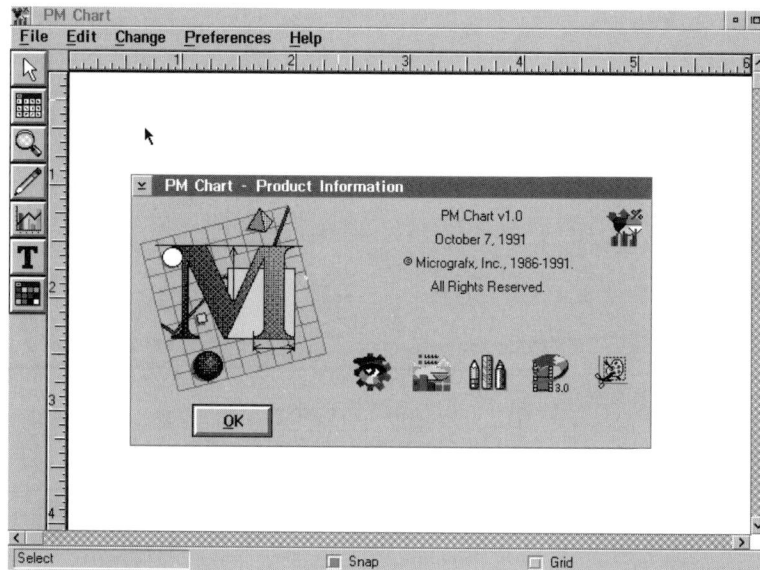

Starting Charts

Use *File/New* to delete the current contents of the worksheet
window. An error message appears if you haven't saved the
changes yet. Click [No] if you don't want to delete the changes.

File/Open displays a window, in which you can load a file. To
save any settings for the next time you load this file, select the
Save option.

PM Chart supports the following file formats:

Format	Description
GRF	Graphic [Charisma] File
DRW	Micrografx Draw File
DAT	[Charisma] Data File
SYLK	Microsoft's Symbolic Link Format
DIF	IBM's Data Interchange Format
XLS	Excel File
WKS	Lotus File
WK1	Lotus File
SPC	ASCII file divided by spaces

Use the *File/Clip Art...* command to load clip art files and insert them into your drawings and diagrams. Then use the Thumbnail button to display a preview of the clip art files.

To avoid the temporary storage and insert the clip art directly into the current drawing, activate the *Auto Paste* option.

If you activate the *Save* option, the settings will be saved for the next time you activate a file.

When you're finished making changes, you can save the file with *File/Save* or *File/Save as...*, if you want to use a different name.

To print a drawing or a diagram, select *File/Print*. You can select whether you want to print the current page (*Page*), a specific portion (*View*), or all pages (*All Pages*).

Use *File/Printer Setup...* to activate the OS/2 printer setup, in which you can set the print quality, the paper size, etc.

Two buttons are located at the bottom of the window. Enable or disable the *Snap to grid* function with *Snap*. *Grid* places a grid over the drawing.

Tool Bar

A tool bar is located to the left of the window. This bar consists of seven symbols, which are located in small squares.

These symbols represent the following functions:

Click on the Arrow symbol to restore your normal selection pointer.

Use the Table symbol to open a chart as a worksheet. From the values entered on it, you can let this tool create a diagram or graph. To move within the table, use [Tab] to move to the right, [Shift] + [Tab] to move to the left, and [↑] and [↓] to move up and down.

To enter numbers or text, move the inverse bar to the appropriate line and type the number or text.

Arithmetic operations aren't available in this worksheet.

Set the current view with the Magnifying glass tool. You can display a preview or a zoomed extract. Clicking on the magnifying glass reveals seven additional fields.

The 1:1 magnifier icon returns you to the default display from every other display mode. The next icon displays a preview. The following icon displays the maximum available area of 4x4 sheets. The next icon displays all the sheets you've worked on so far.

The Pencil icon allows you to draw a rectangle, a rounded rectangle, an ellipse, a line, and arcs. Simply click on the desired drawing icon.

With Chart, you can determine whether the data from the worksheet (table) should be used to create a bar graph, line graph, or a pie chart.

The Text tool helps you insert text in your charts and diagrams.

With the first three icons, you can enter text at a graphic cursor; the middle icon opens a window where you can set the font; and you can adjust the text with the icon to the right.

Color allows you to select colors for the symbols, diagrams, and text.

Mark the corresponding object by clicking on it once, then click on the color field. Select a color from the window that's displayed. When you activate the *Set* option, the color window remains on the screen. You can close it at any time with the [Close] button.

Unlike Windows Paintbrush, the tool bar cannot be removed from the screen.

Block operations

To mark a block with the mouse, select *Edit/Block select*, place the mouse pointer at the beginning of the block, and press the left mouse button while dragging the mouse to the end of the block. Then release the mouse button. The *Edit/Select all* command marks all parts of the drawing as one block.

Press (Del) or select the *Edit/Clear* command to delete a marked block. Use *Edit/Copy* to copy the block into the *Clipboard* and *Edit/Cut* to delete the block.

If a diagram is already in the *Clipboard*, it can be inserted into the current document with *Edit/Paste*. To do this, move the crosshair to the appropriate location and press the left mouse button.

The *Change* menu contains additional commands for block operations. Use *Align* to determine how the marked object should be arranged on the page. A window displays various options.

To combine at least two marked objects, use the *Combine* command. *Change/Combine/Group* combines several objects and *Change/Combine/Ungroup* cancels this grouping.

With *Change/Duplicate* you can easily make copies of an object or a group. To do this, simply mark an object and grasp it with the mouse. Now you can "pull off" a copy of the object and move it to a new location.

To create a horizontal mirror image (flip left to right) of a marked object, use *Change/Flip/Horizontal* and to create a vertical image (flip up and down), use *Change/Flip/Vertical*.

If an object is covered by another object, select *Change/Move to/Back* to move the object that's on top to the background. Use *Change/Move to/Front* to move an object to the foreground.

Because vector graphics are used in *PM Chart*, you can easily rotate objects. To turn an object, mark it with *Edit/Block select*, and activate the *Change/Rotate* command. Crosshairs appear in the center of the marked object.

These crosshairs define the axis around which you turn the object. You can grasp this point with the mouse and move it as desired, to set a different axis. To turn the object, simply grasp it a little closer to the edge and move the mouse accordingly.

Creating a diagram

To create a diagram, first you must enter the values on a spreadsheet.

Click on the second symbol from the top. An empty chart is displayed on the screen. To move the cursor around this chart, use ⟨Tab⟩ to move to the right, ⟨Shift⟩ + ⟨Tab⟩ to move to the left, ⟨↓⟩ to move down, and ⟨↑⟩ to move up.

Use simple values because there isn't a calculation function for this spreadsheet. However, there is a way around this. Mark one or more cells on your spreadsheet and select *Data/Math* from the menu. A window, in which you can enter constants, appears. Then select the arithmetic operation that you want to perform. All marked cells reflect this operation.

For example, to create a diagram, enter the values in the following chart. It provides a quick overview of the number of diskettes you purchased in the first quarter.

```
Diskettes      HDs     DDs
January        30      20
February       20      10
March          60      10
```

Mark the entire field, starting at the upper-left (Diskettes) to the lower-right (10). Click on the diagram symbol. Six additional icons appear. With these icons you can create, from left to right, a vertical-horizontal bar graph, an area graph, a line graph, a pie chart, or a simple chart.

If you click on the first graph type, a window appears. In this window you can specify whether the bar graph should contain *3D* bars and a *Legend*. You can also determine whether a small *Table*, containing the individual values, should appear under the graph.

Additional settings

The *Preferences* menu contains additional settings. In this menu the crosshairs replace the mouse pointer.

Set the paper format, margins, and orientation under *Pages....* *Rulers/Grid...* enables you to set the horizontal and vertical division of the rulers. You can also select *Centimeters* or *Inches* and then select a subdivision of 10 units (millimeters) or 16 units (inches) for the *Rulers*. You can also set the coarseness of the *Grid* from this menu.

Finally, use the *Screen color...* command to select a suitable background color for your graphs.

10.6 PM Terminal

PM Terminal (actually the Softterm Session Manager) is a telecommunications application designed to manage up to 32 connections simultaneously. You can create several connections at the same time. Also, a different terminal emulation can be in effect for each connection.

We'll use an example to explain how to create a connection between *PM Terminal* and a regular BBS (Bulletin Board System).

When *PM Terminal* starts, a window containing the default BBS items appears. Select *Session/Add...* to enter a new BBS. This starts a new entry.

Terminal emulation profile and *Connection path profile* are the important items in the next window. With *Terminal Emulation*, you can use the default setting, ANSI 3.64. If this causes problems, change to DEC VT100.

You must provide correct information about your modem hardware. Under *Connection path profile*, enter the *Modem Port...*. This setting will usually be *COM - Modem...* if you have a regular modem.

Now click on *Add...*. In the dialog window that appears, enter the phone number of your favorite BBS. To be able to use the pulse dialing method, add a [PULSE] entry in front of the phone number. For touch tone dialing, use a [TONE] entry. The entry could look as follows:

```
[TONE] 1-616-698-8106
```

When you're done, click on *Save as...*. A small window requests a *Session name*. In this window, type a brief note about your BBS entry. Save this entry by clicking on *Save*.

To select the BBS, simply double-click on its name. *PM Terminal* will check all your ports if your modem isn't attached to COM Port 1.

When you make a connection, you can work with PM Terminal like you would work with other terminals.

10.7 Pulse

Pulse graphically shows the status of your system.

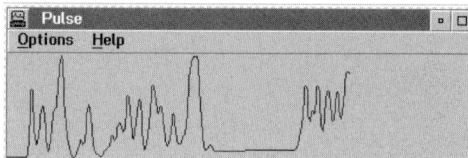

The "heart beat" of OS/2 2.1

The higher the graph, the busier your processor is at any given time. When the graph is near the bottom edge of the window, your processor is practically "idling"; if it's near the top, your processor is fully loaded.

Use the *Options/Background color* and the *Options/Graph color* to set the color scheme of the graph. The *Options* menu also provides additional options that you can enable or disable by simply clicking on them.

Smooth	This smoothes out the graph and creates a "calmer" effect.
Centered	Usually, the graph "pushes" itself through a window. This option causes the graph to be drawn from the center to the right edge.
Freeze screen	Use this command to freeze the graph. However, Pulse continues to work in the background. When you disable *Freeze screen* again, the graph indicates what has been happening in the meantime.
Fill	When this option is active, the surface under the graph is filled with the graph color. The graph itself is then displayed in black.

10.8 Seek and Scan Files

You are probably familiar with the file find program "FF.EXE" from Norton Utilities. *Seek and Scan Files* in OS/2 2.1 is similar to this program.

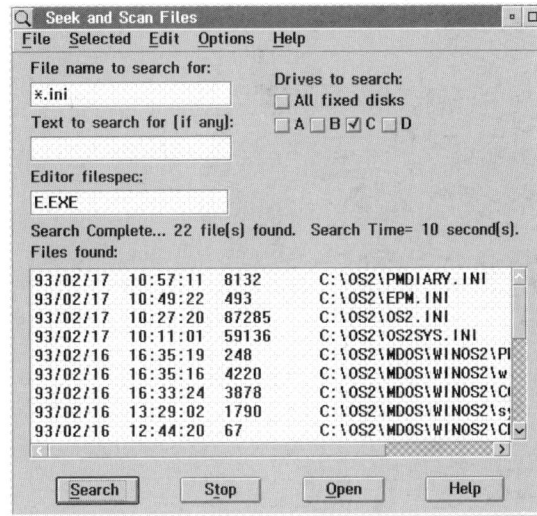

Finding files

After a program is launched, click on *Drives to search* to search the desired drives. *All fixed disks* searches every hard drive. Under *Filenames to search for:*, insert the filenames that you want to find. You can use the wildcards "*", and "?". For example, the following searches for all text files:

```
*.TXT
```

The following searches drives C: and D: for all the files that begin with "CONF":

```
CD:CONF*.*
```

The following would create a list of all files on all drives:

```
*:*.*
```

In the next field, *Text to search for (if any):*, you can enter a text to search for in all the found files. Only those files that contain the sample text will appear on the list. The found text will be displayed in association with the list below the filename. This helps you narrow the search even further.

If you want to use an editor other than the OS/2 2.1 System Editor, E.EXE, enter it under *Editor filespec:*. For example, the following:

```
D:\USER\WORD55\WORD.EXE
```

enables you to use the Word 5.5 word processor to work on texts, if you have Word 5.5 installed on your system in the WORD55 directory.

To launch the editor, simply double-click on the corresponding item or mark it and select (Open).

Click on (Search) to begin the search process. To stop the search, click on (Stop).

Working with the list

Store the resulting list as a file with the *File/Save as...* command so it can be further processed in ASCII format. In the same way, you can copy the list to the *Clipboard* by clicking on *Edit/Copy*. From there, you can insert it in other applications.

The *Edit/Clear list* command deletes the current list. The *Selected* menu provides additional processing capabilities. Use *Selected/Open* to load the Editor or click on the (Open) button near the bottom of the window.

To start the found programs from the list, use the *Selected/Process* command, useful for *.COM, *.EXE, *.BAT, and *.CMD files.

With *Selected/Command...*, it's possible to append a command to a file. For example, if you've searched for and found all the *.BAT files on all the drives, you can enter the command:

```
COPY @ A:\
```

to backup all the batch files on all drives onto a diskette in drive A:. All these files are deleted if you enter:

```
DEL
```

Options

Additional options are located on the *Options* menu. If the *Search subdirectories* option is active, you can also search all subdirectories. The default setting for this option is On.

Enabling the *Display found text* option causes *Seek and Scan Files* to display the corresponding text line that contains the found text. This slows the process because each text is searched to the end.

If *Ignore case* is activated, *Seek and Scan Files* doesn't distinguish between upper and lowercase characters. So, it would find the search string "os/2" even when it's written as "OS/2" in the text.

To expand a list with other search results, first disable *Clear on search*. If this option is activated, each new search deletes an existing list. Save all your settings with *Set defaults*.

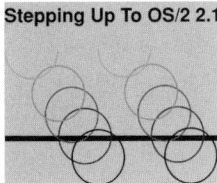

Chapter 11

—— OS/2 2.1 Games ——

Version 2.1 of OS/2 contains several interesting games. You'll find these in the *Games* folder of the *OS/2 System* group.

11.1 Chess

For the *Chess* game, choose the players at the beginning of the program. You can play either the computer or a second player. It's also possible for the computer to play itself. You can select from three levels of difficulty.

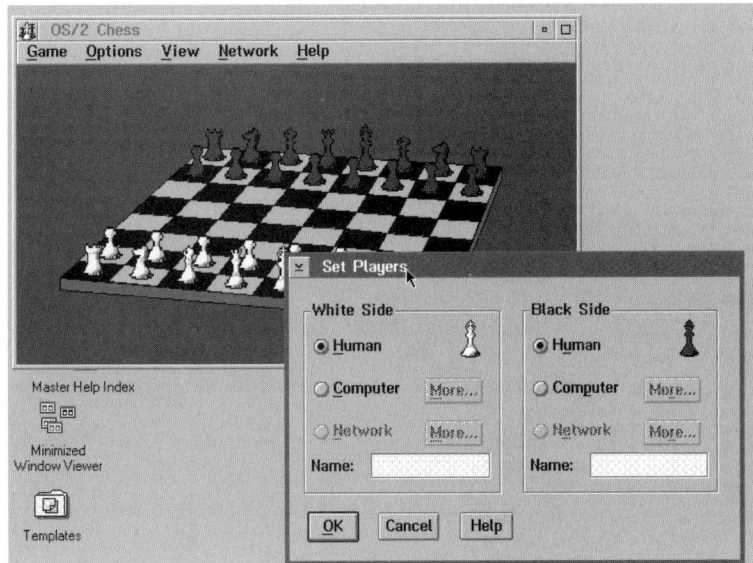

OS/2 2.1 Chess

Move a figure by dragging it with the right mouse button. To castle, move the King to the desired place. The rook is automatically moved to the proper location.

Under *View*, you can obtain information about the game, such as the completed turns and the elapsed time. To change the appearance of the Chess board, use *Options*. You can turn the board, add text, and change its colors. Under *Game*, you can save a session so you can load it again later.

Enter a position to play it yourself or to let the computer solve it by using *Options/Set Positions*. You'll see an empty board with a supply of figures that you can then set up on the board. As soon as you're finished entering the figures, select *Set Positions* again.

11.2 Jigsaw

Jigsaw is a puzzle game that changes any desired BMP file into a jigsaw puzzle. For this game, you must load a picture. The following directory contains the OS/2 logo bitmap:

C:\OS2\BITMAP

Use *Options/Size* to adjust the size of the puzzle pieces. The game will then display a complete picture. To break up the picture, use *Options/Jumble*.

Now you must fit the individual pieces back together. Move each piece with the right mouse button. When a piece is placed in the proper location, the computer beeps.

11.3 Cat and Mouse

Cat and Mouse isn't actually a game. Instead, it's a graphic demonstration that helps you learn how to use the mouse.

In this program, a cat chases your mouse pointer. Use *Speed* and *Step* to adjust the cat's speed and pace. *Play time* sets the games duration.

The (Register) button saves these values for the next time you play the game. The (Hide) button clears the screen. Then the cat runs away from the mouse. Click on the cat to return to your windows.

11.4 Scramble

Scramble is a tile game that you've probably seen on other computer systems. Place the mouse over the tile you want to move and click once with the left or the right mouse button. The tile slides into the empty space.

You can select different patterns under *Game/Open*. With *Game/Scramble*, the computer mixes up all the tiles again.

11.5 Reversi

This is the same game that's included in Windows 3.0. It's played the same way except that this version seems to be a little more complicated.

Under *Options*, you can decide whether your two game pieces should be arranged horizontally or diagonally. Select either *Diagonal Start* or *Horizontal Start*.

11.6 Klondike

This game is called *Solitaire* under Windows. However, this version is a little more attractive and has an autoplay function.

On autoplay, the computer plays the game itself. This proves that *Solitaire* is a game of chance because usually even the computer doesn't win.

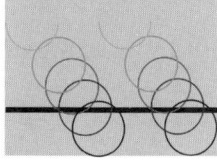

Chapter 12

Batch Files and REXX

A batch file contains a series of commands that a program follows in sequence. These commands are executed as if they had appeared, one after the other, on the command line.

Under OS/2 you can create batch files as you have under DOS, with your favorite ASCII Editor or even the *OS/2 System Editor*. To create short batch files, type:

```
COPY CON: HELLO.BAT
```

to start the batch file entry. When you've entered all the commands, type:

```
<Ctrl> + Z or F6
```

to end the entry. The current directory will then copy the text to the file under the name you gave it.

Most likely, you've already created batch files. It's possible to use your DOS batch files under OS/2.

If the batch files have a .BAT extension, they'll always be executed in DOS boxes. OS/2 executes only batch files ending in .CMD. You can even rename your batch files to fit OS/2 conventions.

The two new commands under OS/2 are:

```
SETLOCAL
```

and:

```
ENDLOCAL
```

Use SETLOCAL to save the entire environment. OS/2 stores the current drive, the current directory, and all environment variables. Use ENDLOCAL to restore these values.

You can write batch files that run with a new path for part of the time (PATH), for example, without having to put the current path into temporary storage.

```
PATH
SETLOCAL
PATH A:\
PATH
...
ENDLOCAL
PATH
```

This example demonstrates how SETLOCAL and ENDLOCAL are used.

OS/2 contains a much more powerful language than the batch file commands of DOS. This program is called the OS/2 Procedures Language 2/REXX, or REXX for short.

12.1 REXX Basics

REXX is a combination of a kind of BASIC and a powerful extension of the well-known batch file programming. You can use not only REXX commands, but also every OS/2 command from the command line.

REXX programs run only under the OS/2 Shell and must have the extension ".CMD". The first line of every REXX program is a remark in the following form:

```
/*This is a REXX program */
```

You can create REXX programs with any ASCII editor. For example, from the command line, you can enter:

```
E HELLO.CMD
```

to open an *OS/2 System Editor* window to create or modify the file named HELLO.CMD.

12.2 Writing Programs

The following sample program demonstrates the capabilities of REXX. This program, called HELLO.CMD, asks you for your name and then says hello.

```
/* Hello, world! for OS/2 2.1 */
SAY "Hello OS/2 world!"
```

```
SAY "Please enter your name"
PULL name
IF name = ""
THEN say "Hello, stranger..."
ELSE SAY "Hello" name
EXIT
```

If you've programmed in BASIC, Pascal, or dBase/Clipper, you should be able to learn REXX programming very quickly.

With REXX you'll be able to call over 70 internal functions. These include functions for string and number operations, for generating sounds, for stating time and date, for file management, and much more.

To experiment with REXX, start REXXTRY.CMD from the command line by typing:

```
PMREXX REXXTRY
```

You'll see a window where you can not only run REXX programs, but also test how individual statements interact.

REXX Interpreter

To learn about REXX, open *REXX Information* in the *Information* folder into another window alongside PMREXX. Now you can try some programming in PMREXX and learn about REXX with *REXX Information*. The following:

```
SAY 4 + 4
```

provides information about how many bits are in a byte. The multiplication-before-addition rule applies here. So the following:

```
SAY 2 + 8 * 5
```

results in 42 instead of 50.

Variables are very easy to enter:

```
Processor = 386
Better = Processor + 100
```

Now when you enter:

```
SAY Processor
```

you get the result "386". If you enter:

```
SAY Better
```

the result is "486".

It's also possible to use strings (character strings) with REXX. The following:

```
SAY WORDS('This sentence contains four words.')
```

results in "5". The following is more complicated:

```
SAY REVERSE('?redo ,sdrow ruof sniatnoc ecnetnes sihT')
```

To do more interesting things, such as viewing the system time and date, you can use both of the REXX commands:

```
SAY DATE
SAY TIME()
```

To create a tone of 440 Hertz of 100 millisecond duration, simply use:

```
CALL BEEP 440,100
```

With REXX, you can create loops, multiple choices, and even a few original procedures.

A loop that creates a sound that's similar to the sound of the Pacman game looks like this:

```
/* Sound */
DO i=200 to 500 by 20
CALL BEEP i,2
END
```

Finally, we'll demonstrate how to calculate factorials (FAC.CMD). This example also shows how to take a parameter from the command line (ARG x):

```
/* calculate factors */
ARG x
SAY x"! = " factor(x)
EXIT

factor : PROCEDURE
 ARG n
IF n=0 THEN RETURN 1
RETURN factor(n-1)*n
```

Activate this program with a parameter that's actually the number for which you want to calculate the factorial. The following:

```
FAC 5
```

calculates the factor of 5 (namely (1*2*3*4*5) = 120).

12.3 Launching Programs

Launch REXX programs as you launch other batch files, by entering the filename. If you want, you can also enter parameters on the command line, providing the REXX program uses them.

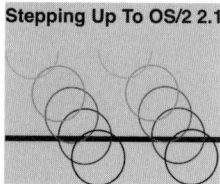

Appendix A

Tips For Using OS/2

If you want to start using OS/2 quickly, the following tips can help. We compiled these as we worked with OS/2.

- Instead of [Alt] + [Esc], you now use [Alt] + [Home] to toggle between a DOS window and the full screen.

- Jump to an entry in the list boxes by typing the first letter of the entry.

- The *Window List* (Task Manager in Windows) no longer appears on the empty Desktop when you double-click. Instead, you must press both mouse buttons simultaneously over the OS/2 Desktop.

- The Accessories Group in Windows corresponds to the *Productivity* folder under OS/2 System.

- You no longer need to load the Print Manager. It doesn't even exist as an external program. Instead, simply open the printer object by double-clicking. You can then delete and pause print jobs in their Object menus.

- Click the right mouse button on an icon to display the Object menu.

- The Shell (DOS Window) is in the OS/2 System program group in the *Command Prompts* folder.

- Install a Windows printer driver with the help of the Windows Control Panel. This driver is then available to Windows applications. Connect the driver to the OS2.LPTx port by starting *WIN-OS/2 Full Screen*, which is in the OS/2 System program group in the *Command Prompts* folder.

- You can select several icons with a rubber band. To do this, hold down the left mouse button and drag it across the screen.

- You'll find the PIF settings in the Object menu of the program under *Open/Settings* on the *Session* page. *DOS Settings* displays additional options.

- OS/2 2.1 no longer has an AUTOEXEC.BAT. All settings are made in the CONFIG.SYS file. The AUTOEXEC.BAT is used only for the DOS windows.

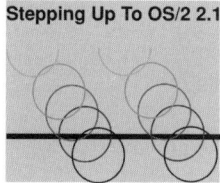

Appendix B

Command Reference

This section describes all the OS/2 2.1 commands. Although the commands basically work as they do in MS-DOS, most have been updated. Usually there are new parameters or other minor changes. For example, the TYPE command now works with wildcards.

Command	Explanation
ANSI	ANSI emulation on and off
APPEND	Search path for data
ASSIGN	Change the drive label
ATTRIB	Change file attributes
AUTOFAIL	Display error condition message
BACKUP	Create a backup
BASEDEV	Install Base Device Drivers
BOOT	Select an operating system
BREAK	Check for Ctrl+Break keys
BUFFERS	Determines number of disk buffers
CACHE	Writes memory cache to disk
CALL	Start a batch file
CD	Change directories
CHCP	Change the Code Page
CHDIR	Change directories
CHKDSK	Check diskettes
CLS	Clear screen
CMD	Start command interpreter
CODEPAGE	Prepare the Code Pages
COMMAND	Open DOS window
COMP	Compare files
COPY	Copy files
COUNTRY	Identify country information

Command	Explanation
CREATEDD	Prepare Core-Dump
DATE	Set date
DDINSTALL	Install Auto Device Drivers
DEBUG	Start debugger
DEL	Delete file
DETACH	Start program
DEVICE	Install device drivers
DEVICEHIGH	DOS driver into upper memory
DEVINFO	Prepare for code page switching
DIR	Display directory
DISKCACHE	Allocate cache storage blocks
DISKCOMP	Compare diskettes
DISKCOPY	Copy diskettes
DOSKEY	History buffer for DOS
DOS UMB	Set DOS upper memory block
DPATH	Set search path
EAUTIL	Manage extended attributes
ECHO	Output messages
ENDLOCAL	Restore safe environment
ERASE	Delete files
EXIT	Exit command interpreter
EXTPROC	Define command interpreter
FCBS	Use file control blocks
FDISK	Partition disk
FDISKPM	Partition disk
FILES	Set maximum number of files
FIND	Search for text
FOR	Perform commands more than once
FORMAT	Format diskettes and hard drives
FSACCESS	Change File System access
FSFILTER	Access HPFS from DOS
GOTO	Jump to a batch file
GRAFTABL	Display character set
HELP	Help on a problem or command
IF	Decisions in a batch file
IFS	Install File System
IOPL	Allow Input/Output Privilege
JOIN	Convert drive to path
KEYB	Change keyboard layout

Command	Explanation
KEYS	History buffer
LABEL	Rename diskettes
LASTDRIVE	Set last accessible drive
LIBPATH	Identify Dynamic Link Libraries
LH	Load program into High memory
MAKEINI	Create new INI file
MAXWAIT	Set Maximum wait
MEM	Output memory map
MEMMAN	Select memory allocation
MD	Make a directory
MODE	Configure ports
MORE	Display file page by page
MOVE	Move file
PATCH	Input CSDs
PATH	Change search path
PAUSE	Wait for keystroke
PAUSEONEROR	Pause CONFIG.SYS messages
PICVIEW	Display meta files
PMREXX	Interactive REXX programs
PRINT	Print files
PRINTMONBUFSIZE	Set printer port buffer size
PRIORITY	Schedule threads
PRIORITY_DISK_IO	Set disk priority
PROMPT	Change prompt
PROTECTONLY	Select Operating environments
PROTSHELL	Load user shell
PSTAT	Display process status
RD	Remove directory
RECOVER	Recover files
REN	Rename files
REPLACE	Replace files
RESTORE	Restore backup files
RMSIZE	Specify DOS environment size
RUN	Start System program
SET	Set environment variable
SETBOOT	Control Boot Manager
SETLOCAL	Save environment
SHELL	Install command processor
SHIFT	Shift parameters

Command	Explanation
SORT	Sort files
SPOOL	Configure printer
START	Start program
SUBST	Substitute drive
SWAPPATH	Specify swap file
SYSLEVEL	Display version number
SYSLOG	Error log
THREADS	Set number of independent actions
TIME	Set time
TIMESLICE	Allocate Wait time
TRACE	Trace API calls
TRACEBUF	Set Trace buffer size
TRACEFMT	Trace format
TREE	Show directory tree
TYPE	Display file
UNDELETE	Recover file
UNPACK	Decompress files
VER	Display version number
VERIFY	Verify on and off
VIEW	Show ReadMe's
VMDISK	Create DOS image file
VOL	Display volume
XCOPY	Copy files

ANSI

Protected mode

Description

Switches the ANSI driver on and off.

It doesn't matter whether the ANSI driver is in the CONFIG.SYS file. This driver handles only the DOS windows.

By default, ANSI emulation is active. If you enter the command without any parameters, the current status will be output.

Syntax

```
ANSI Option
```

ON   Switches ANSI emulation on.
OFF   Switches ANSI emulation off.

APPEND

Real mode

Description

Use APPEND to define a search path for data. This is used only in Real mode. In Protected mode, the DPATH setting in the CONFIG.SYS file is used.

If you enter the command without any parameters, the current status will be output.

Syntax

```
APPEND Path Option
```

Path

Specify the search path for the data here. The search path has the same structure as the normal path. All the directories are separated by semicolons.

Option

/E   This option saves the search path in the DOS environment. Then you can use SET to modify this path.

          You can use this option only the first time you start APPEND.

/Path:On

          If you specify a file with a complete path, this directory will be searched first. If the file isn't found there, the other directories are also searched.

/Path:Off

          Append will function only if you specify a file without a path.

ASSIGN

Real mode

Description

Use this command to assign a different volume to a drive. You can also create new drives with this command. However, such a pseudo-drive doesn't have any properties.

So, the commands that respond to the properties of a drive won't function on a pseudo drive. The following lists the commands that don't work with assigned drives:

Command	Action
CHKDSK	Check diskette
DISKCOMP	Compare diskettes
DISKCOPY	Copy diskette
FORMAT	Format diskette/hard drive
JOIN	Assign a path to a drive
LABEL	Rename diskette/hard drive
PRINT	Print files
RECOVER	Recover diskette/hard drive
RESTORE	Restore backup copies
SUBST	Assign a drive to a directory

Syntax

```
ASSIGN Drive1 = Drive2
```

Drive1

The drive to reassign.

Drive2

The new drive to which input and output will be redirected.

NOTE

Protected mode programs and family API programs cannot access drives linked with ASSIGN and SUBST.

If you specify the command without any parameters, all the drive assignments will be canceled.

ATTRIB

Protected and Real mode

Description

Use ATTRIB to change the file attributes. You cannot access extended attributes with this command.

Syntax

```
APPEND Option1 Path Option2
```

Option1

+R   File is read only. File can no longer be written to or deleted.

-R   You can also write to the file.

+A This file will not be included in the next backup, since it has already been backed up.

-A This file has been changed since the last backup, so it must be backed up.

+S This file is labeled a system file. Many commands refuse access to this file.

-S System attribute is canceled.

+H File is invisible (hidden) and will be ignored by DIR, COPY.

-H File is no longer hidden.

Path

Specify the file whose attributes you want to change here. You can use wildcards.

Option2

/S This option includes all subdirectories.

AUTOFAIL

Protected mode

Description

This command is entered in the CONFIG.SYS file to enable the display error messages.

Syntax

```
AUTOFAIL Option
```

Option

NO A window displays information about the error condition. This is the default.

YES Only the error code is displayed.

BACKUP

Protected mode

Description

Use this command to make backup copies of your files and hard drives. You can restore the backups with the Restore command.

BACKUP doesn't back up hidden files or system files. It also doesn't back up any open DLLs. It backs up only those files to which you have access rights. If another user opened them exclusively, you cannot back them up.

BACKUP includes extended attributes in the backup.

Syntax

```
BACKUP Source Target Option
```

Source

Specify the file you want to back up here. You can also use wildcards. If you specify a drive without a path, the command backs up the entire drive:

```
BACKUP C: A:
```

Target

Specify the target of the backup here. Usually you use one of the disk drives (A: or B:). You could also specify a hard drive, however. If you're on a network, you could save yourself the trouble of changing diskettes by placing the backups on the network.

Option

/L:File   Places a log file of the backup process in the specified file. If you don't specify a filename, the BACKUP.LOG file will be used in the root directory of the source drive. The date and time the backup was created are written to this file. The log file also has information about which files are located on which diskettes.

/D:dd-mm-yy
    Backs up only files that have been changed after the specified date.

/T:hh:mm:ss
    Backs up only those files that have been changed after the specified time. Usually combined with /D.

/M   Backs up files that have been changed since the last backup (i.e., the archive bit is cleared).

/A   Adds the files being backed up to an existing backup copy. The old files aren't deleted or overwritten.

/F:n   Formats the diskettes with n kilobytes if necessary. The values 360, 720, 1200, 1440, and 2880 can be used.

/S   Includes subdirectories in the backup.

BASEDEV

Protected and Real mode

Description

Installs a base device driver from the CONFIG.SYS file. Used to load support for hard drives, diskettes, printers and other devices.

Syntax

```
BASEDEV= Option
```

Option

The device driver. A path or drive can't be entered in this statement.

BOOT

Protected and Real mode

Description

Use this command to switch between OS/2 2.1 and DOS. DOS and OS/2 must be on the same hard drive (dual boot installation) to use this command. For more information, refer to Chapter 1.

Syntax

```
BOOT Option
```

Option

/OS2   Switches to OS/2 2.1 and reboots the computer.

/DOS   Switches to DOS and reboots the computer.

BREAK

Real mode

Description

Checks for the [Ctrl] and Break key combination.

NOTE

Enter the BREAK command at the DOS prompt to check the current status. BREAK can be entered in the CONFIG.SYS file, the AUTOEXEC.BAT file or at the command prompt.

Syntax

```
BREAK Parameter
```

Parameter

You can turn BREAK checking ON or OFF.

BUFFERS

Protected and Real mode

Description

This command sets the number of 512 byte buffers used by the system to read and write disk blocks. This command is used in the CONFIG.SYS file.

Syntax

```
BUFFERS= Parameter
```

Parameter

Parameters are the number of 512 byte blocks of memory to use.

CACHE

Protected and Real mode

Description

This command specifies how the HPFS writes data to the disk. This command is used in a RUN command in the CONFIG.SYS file.

Syntax

```
CACHE= Options
```

Options

/LAZY:state	Specifies when disk cache is written.
/MAXAGE:time	Specifies amount of time before writes.
/DISKIDLE:time	Specified disk idle time.
/BUFFERIDLE:time	Sets cache buffer idle time.

CALL

Protected and Real mode

Description

Calls a second batch file from a batch file and then returns to the first batch file.

NOTE

If possible, don't have a batch file call itself. This could cause stack overflow.

Syntax

```
CALL Parameter
```

Parameter

You can pass parameters to the file you're calling. These are available under %1, %2, %3, etc.

CHCP

Protected and Real mode

Description

This command sets the code page character set. This command is used in the CONFIG.SYS file. Type this command with no parameters to display the current code page number.

Syntax

```
CHCP Parameter
```

Parameter

Parameter is the code page number.

CD or CHDIR

Protected and Real mode

Description

This command changes the current directory.

If you specify the command without any parameters, the current directory is output.

Syntax

```
CD Option
CHDIR Option
```

Option

Path   Specify the path here.

..   Changes to the next highest directory, if you're already in the root directory, nothing happens.

\   Changes to the root directory of the current drive.

CHKDSK

Protected and Real mode

Description

CHKDSK checks and repairs the logical structure of a diskette/hard drive.

This command automatically recognizes the file system being used (HPFS or FAT) and displays a message indicating this.

Under DOS, this command also outputs information about the memory. However, you can also obtain this report with MEM. CHKDSK doesn't work with ASSIGN, SUBST, or JOIN.

> **NOTE**
>
> The diskette/hard drive cannot be used when CHKDSK is running. No files can be opened. This is a problem for the boot hard drive. In order to check it, you must boot from a diskette. To do this, insert the first OS/2 2.1 installation diskette and reboot the computer. As soon as you're prompted for the second diskette, insert this also.
>
> After that, the text screen appears. In the bottom line of the screen you'll see "ESC - To cancel". Press (Esc) to go to the OS/2 2.1 command line. From there you can start CHKDSK from a floppy diskette. You'll find this program on the third diskette.

From time to time, sectors are labeled as reserved, but are not being used in a file. These sectors are saved in the FILExxxx.CHK file. The value for xxxx increases in ascending order as the files are created. You can then check these files and save data.

Extended attributes are stored in the EAxxxx.CHK files. The FILExxxx.CHK and EAxxxx.CHK files go together.

When you start the computer, OS/2 2.1 can determine whether the computer was simply switched off or the power supply was interrupted. It automatically checks the file systems and corrects errors. This can slow down the boot process. But a system like OS/2 2.1 must be able to rely on a consistent file system.

Syntax

```
CHKDSK Path Option
```

Path

Specify the drive you want checked here. If you specify a file, only this file will be checked. You can use wildcards when specifying files.

Option

/F:n   Any errors found will be corrected. If this parameter isn't included in the command, CHKDSK will find errors, but won't correct them.

You can only specify n in protected mode. This parameter determines which errors are corrected. 0 indicates no corrections. 1 corrects errors in the directory. 2 searches for sectors that are reserved, but not registered in the directory. 3 searches all the empty areas of a hard drive for data.

/V   Displays a list of all checked files.

/C   Recovers files only if the file system was found to be damaged at start-up. You can use this parameter only in Protected mode.

CLS

Protected and Real mode

Description

Clears the screen.

Syntax

```
CLS
```

CMD

Protected mode

Description

Starts a new command processor in Protected mode. Use EXIT to exit this command interpreter.

Syntax

```
CMD Path Option
```

Path

Specify the contents of the COMSPEC variables here. If you don't specify this parameter, the path of the current command interpreter is used.

Option

/Q   This command interpreter doesn't produce any output on the screen.

/S   Doesn't allow any interruptions from Ctrl + C.

/K:"Command"

Starts a new command interpreter and immediately executes the command. The new command interpreter isn't terminated.

/C:"Command"

Starts a new command interpreter and immediately executes the command. The new command interpreter is immediately terminated.

CODEPAGE

Protected and Real mode

Description

This command sets the code page character set. This command is used in the CONFIG.SYS file. You must also include the DEVINFO statements for both code pages in the CONFIG.SYS files.

Syntax

```
CODEPAGE Parameter1, Parameter2
```

Parameter1

Primary code page.

Parameter2

Secondary code page.

COMMAND

Real mode

Description

Starts a new command processor in Real mode. You can use EXIT to exit this command interpreter as long as you didn't use /P to make it permanent. In this case, you must close the entire DOS window.

Syntax

```
COMMAND Path Option
```

Path

Specify the contents of the COMSPEC variables here. If you don't specify this parameter, the path of the current command interpreter is used.

Option

/P   The new command interpreter is resident in the system. You cannot use Exit to exit the system.

> **WARNING** | Don't use /P under OS/2 2.1. You cannot use EXIT to exit a primary command interpreter.

/E:n   Defines the size of the environment. Specify the size in bytes. Set a high value if you frequently work with batch files and environment variables.

/K Command
   Starts a new command interpreter and immediately performs the command. The new command interpreter is not terminated.

/C Command
   Starts a new command interpreter and immediately performs the command. The new command interpreter is immediately terminated.

COMP

Protected and Real mode

Description

Use this command to compare two files.

Syntax

```
COMP File1 File2
```

File1 File2

Specify the two files you want compared here; wildcards are allowed.

If you don't specify File1 or File2, COMP will prompt you for the filenames individually.

COPY

Protected and Real mode

Description

Use this command to copy files. You can also use this command to combine several files into one.

Since the parameters for both operations are different, we'll describe them separately.

Copying files

COPY copies the extended attributes of a file or directory.

If the target drive doesn't support extended attributes, an error message, indicating that the extended attributes were lost, appears on the screen. The command then copies the files without the extended attributes.

Syntax

```
COPY Source Option1 Target Option2
```

Source

Specify the file to be copied here; wildcards are permitted.

Option1

/A   The files are treated as ASCII files. In other words, the file is copied only until the first EOF appears.

/B   The files are treated as binary files. Accordingly, all EOFs are copied. This is the default setting.

Target

Specify the target here. Usually the target is a directory or a drive. The files are then copied to the target.

Option2

/A   Adds an EOF to the end of the file.

/B   Does not add an EOF to the file. This is the default setting.

/V   Verifies the file. After copying, the data is read once again and compared with the source data. If the two don't match, Copy displays an error message.

/F   Some programs store important data in the extended attributes. The files might be useless without their extended attributes. Use this parameter to prevent files with extended attributes from being copied to non HPFS diskettes.

Merging files

You can use the COPY command to combine several files into a single file. A different syntax is used to do this.

Syntax

```
COPY Src1+Src2+Source... Option1 Target Option2
```

Source

Specify the various source files here; you can use wildcards.

Option1

/A   The files are treated as ASCII files. The file is copied only until the first EOF appears.

/B   Files are treated as binary files. Accordingly, EOFs are also copied. This is the default setting.

Target

Specify the target here. The source files are combined in this file.

If you don't specify a target, the first source file is used as a target.

Option2

/A   Adds an EOF to the end of the file.

/B   Doesn't add an EOF to the end of the file. This is the default setting.

/V   Verifies the file. After the write process, the data is read again and compared with the source data. If they don't match, an error message appears on the screen.

/F   Some programs store important data in the extended attributes. Without their extended attributes, the files might be useless. Use this parameter to prevent files with extended attributes from being copied to non HPFS diskettes/hard drives.

COUNTRY

Protected and Real mode

Description

This command sets the country information, including the time and date format, decimal separator, character sort sequence, and character map. This command is used in the CONFIG.SYS file.

Syntax

```
COUNTRY Parameter1, Parameter2
```

Parameter1

Three digit country value.

Parameter2

File that contains the country specific information.

CREATEDD

Protected mode

Description

This command is important only to system developers. OS/2 2.1 gives you the option of creating a complete memory dump. During the process, the entire physical memory is saved. You can then analyze the memory. UNIX developers refer to this as "core dumped".

Use the CREATEDD command to prepare the diskettes for a core dump. You must prepare only the first diskette. The remaining diskettes just need to be formatted.

WARNING | CREATEDD and core dump delete all the data on the diskettes.

Use the key combination Ctrl + Alt + Num Lock + Num Lock to perform the core dump. Press Num Lock twice.

WARNING | During a core dump, programs aren't ended, files aren't closed, or print jobs aren't saved. The computer stops in its current state.

You can also perform an automatic core dump. To do this, add the setting:

```
TrapDump=On
```

to the CONFIG.SYS. A core dump will be produced every time an error, which would ordinarily force an application to end, occurs.

Syntax

```
CREATEDD Drive
```

Drive

Specify one of your disk drives here (either A: or B:).

NOTE | The core dump itself always occurs on drive A:.

DATE

Protected and Real mode

Description

Use this command to reset the date on the computer.

If you specify the command without any parameters, the current date appears, followed by a prompt for a new date.

Syntax

```
DATE
```

Date

Specify the current date here. The format depends on the Country setting in the CONFIG.SYS.

In the United States, for example, the date is usually specified in the following format:

```
Month/Day/Year
```

For the year, 00-79 is interpreted as 2000 to 2079 and 80-99 is interpreted as 1980 to 1999. However, you could also use four digits to specify the year.

DDINSTALL

Real mode

Description

Provides a method of installing device drivers after OS/2 has been started. These device drive files are located on Device Support diskettes, which contain .DDP (Device Drive Profile) files that control the installation of the drivers. If the installation is successful, the CONFIG.SYS file is updated and you should reboot your computer.

Syntax

```
DDINSTALL File
```

File

This file is loaded by the DDINSTALL program.

DEBUG

Real mode

Description

Starts the DOS debug program.

Syntax

```
DEBUG File
```

File

This file is loaded into the debug program.

Debug program commands

?	Outputs a list of all debug commands.
A	Starts the assembler. The assembler doesn't process any 286/386 commands.
C	Compares two areas of memory.
D	Displays a memory dump.
E	Writes data to an area of memory.
F	Fills a memory area with a value.
G	Starts the loaded program.
H	Provides a hexadecimal calculator.
I	Gets a value from an IO port.
L	Loads a file or a sector.
M	Copies a memory block.
N	Specify the start parameters for a program here. This command also defines the file for the L and W commands.
O	Writes a value to an IO port.
P	Runs a loop or procedure.
Q	Quits the debug program.
R	Outputs the register assignments of the processor.
S	Searches an area of memory.
T	Executes the program step-by-step and displays the register for each command.
U	Unassembles a memory area.
W	Writes the file or sector back to disk.
XA	Requests expanded memory.
XD	Releases expanded memory.
XM	Inserts an EMS page.
XS	Outputs a status report of the EMS driver.

DEL

Protected and Real mode

Description

Deletes a file. Use RMDIR to delete directories.

Syntax

```
DEL File File File ... Option
```

File

Specifies the file to be deleted. Wildcards are permitted. You can specify this parameter more than once to delete several files with one command.

Option

/P   Prompts you to confirm deletion for each file.

/N   Suppresses the security prompt when you delete all the files of a directory.

DETACH

Protected mode

Description

Starts a program in the background. This program cannot send output to the screen or receive keyboard input.

If this cannot be avoided, you can intercept output and input with file redirection.

When you start the program, its PID (Process Identification Number) is output. The program is managed in the system under this number.

Syntax

```
DETACH File
```

File

This program is started. Only protected mode programs can be started in this way.

DEVICE

Protected and Real mode

Description

This statement allows you to set up OS/2 devices. This command is used in the CONFIG.SYS file.

Syntax

```
DEVICE= Parameter
```

Parameter

ANSI.SYS, COM.SYS, EGA.SYS, EXTDSKDD.SYS, LOG.SYS, MOUSE.SYS, PMDD.SYS, POINTDD.SYS, TOUCH.SYS, VDISK.SYS, VEMM.SYS, VXMS.SYS

DEVICEHIGH

Real mode

Description

This command loads the DOS driver into available upper memory block.

Syntax

```
DEVICEHIGH= Driver
```

Driver

Driver is a DOS device driver.

DEVINFO

Protected and Real mode

Description

This command prepares a device for code page switching. Separate DEVINFO statements are required for each device. This command is used in the CONFIG.SYS files.

Syntax

```
DEVINFO Parameter
```

Parameter

KDB   Prepare a keyboard for code page switching.

SCR   Prepare a display screen for code page switching.

LPT#   Prepare a printer for code page switching.

DIR

Protected and Real mode

Description

Displays the directory of a diskette/hard drive. If you specify the command without any parameters, all the files of the current directory are displayed.

Files with a set hidden attribute aren't included in the display.

On an HPFS partition, the display differs slightly from the ordinary display under DOS. The following information appears in the display:

1. Date of the last change.

2. Time of the last change.

3.   Size of the file in bytes or <DIR>.

4. Size of the file's extended attributes.

5. The filename.

You can place parameters for the DIR command in the DIRCMD environment variable. These parameters are then used as the default setting. This variable is used in both Protected mode and in Real mode.

Syntax

```
DIR File Option
```

File

If you don't specify this parameter, the command works with * in the current directory.

Otherwise, specify the usual paths and filenames here.

Option

/W   Displays only file and directory names. The entries are arranged side by side. The number of files placed next to each other depends on the longest filename.

/F   Displays the file and directory names with their complete paths.

NOTE   You cannot use /W and /F together.

/P   Pauses at each full screen page and waits for you to press a key.

/N   Forces the HPFS output format on a FAT diskette/hard drive.

/A:x   Uses attributes for x. Only entries with the matching attribute are displayed. The default file attributes are allowed (H, -H, S, -S, A, -A, R, -R). In addition, you could specify the D parameter, which causes only the directories to be displayed. Specify -D to display only files.

/B   Brief mode displays only data and directory names.

/O:x   Orders or sorts the display. You can use the following values for x:

Value	Sort order
N	Alphabetically by filename
E	Alphabetically by file extensions
D	By date, in ascending order
S	By file size, in ascending order
G	First directories, then files

Use a minus sign (-) to reverse the sorting sequence.

/R   Displays both the real filename and the HPFS filename on a FAT diskette/hard drive. This is stored in the extended attributes.

/S   Displays all the subdirectories.

/L   Displays the information in lowercase letters.

DISKCACHE

Protected and Real mode

Description

This command is used to specify the number of 1024 byte blocks to use for control information of the disk cache. The default is 64. This command is used in the CONFIG.SYS files.

Syntax

```
DISKCACHE= Number, Parameters
```

Number

Number   The number of 1024 byte blocks to use.

Parameter

,LW   Specifies whether Lazy Write is used.

,T   Threshold size for number of sectors in cache (4-128).

,AC:x   Autochecks the drive (x, C-Z) at startup.

DISKCOMP

Protected and Real mode

Description

Compares two diskettes with each other.

Syntax

```
DISKCOMP Drive Drive
```

Drive

The diskettes in both drives are compared.

DISKCOPY

Protected and Real mode

Description

Copies complete diskettes.

Syntax

```
DISKCOPY Source Target
```

Source

This diskette is copied to the target.

Target

The data from the source diskette are copied to the diskette in this drive.

DOSKEY

Real mode

Description

Provides options for editing a line in the DOS command interpreter. Also manages a history buffer. This program is usually loaded in the AUTOEXEC.BAT file.

Syntax

```
DOSKEY Option
```

Option

/ Reinstall

Installs another instance of the program in memory.

/ BufSize=x

Sets the size of the history buffer. Ordinarily the size is set at 512 bytes.

/M   Displays all defined macros.

/H   Displays the history buffer.

/Overstrike

> Overstrike mode used in the command line.

/Insert

> Insert mode used in the command line.

DOS

Real mode

Description

> This command is used to specify whether the DOS kernel is loaded into the High Memory Area or HMA. You can also specify whether DOS applications or the operating system controls the upper memory blocks or UMBs. This command is used in the CONFIG.SYS files.

Syntax

```
DOS= Parameter1, Parameter2
```

Parameter1

> HIGH   The DOS kernel is loaded into the High Memory Area.
>
> LOW   The DOS kernel is not loaded into the High Memory Area.

Parameter2

> UMB   The DOS kernel is loaded into the Upper Memory Block.
>
> NOUMB The DOS kernel is not loaded into the Upper Memory Block.

DPATH

Protected mode

Description

> Use DPATH to define a search path for data. This is used only in Protected mode. The DPATH setting is set with the SET command in OS/2 sessions.
>
> DPATH without any parameters will display the current value.

Syntax

```
DPATH Path ;
```

Path

> Specify the search path for the data here. The search path has the same structure as the normal path. All the directories are separated by semicolons.

Option

;   Clears the DPATH environment variable.

EAUTIL

Protected and Real mode

Description

This program saves the extended attributes in an extra file or restores them from the file.

For example, if your tape drive software cannot work with extended attributes, you extract the extended attributes in an extra file before backing up. When you recover the backup, you can restore the extended attributes from the extra file.

Syntax

```
EAUTIL Source Backup-File Option
```

Source

Back up the extended attributes from this file. You can also specify entire directories and use wildcards.

Backup-file

Save the extended attributes in this file. This parameter is optional. If you don't specify this file, the extended attributes are saved to a file with the same name as the original. This file is placed in the EAS directory, which is on the same level as the source directory.

Option

/S   Backs up the extended attributes to a file. In the process, the extended attributes are deleted.

/R   Replaces an existing backup file.

/J   Recovers the extended attributes with the help of the backup file. The extended attributes are deleted from the backup file.

/O   Overwrites the current extended attributes of the file with those of the backup file.

/M   Adds the extended attributes from the backup file to the current extended attributes of the file.

/P   When a backup file is created, the extended attributes of the file are preserved.

ECHO

Protected and Real mode

Description

Displays a message on the screen. Also switches the display of commands in a batch file on and off. The current status is displayed if you specify the command without any parameters.

Syntax

    ECHO Option

Option

On   Switches the command display on.

Off   Switches the command display off.

Text   Displays the text.

ENDLOCAL

Protected mode

Description

The SETLOCAL command creates a copy of all environment variables. After that, you can make any changes to the variables. The ENDLOCAL command then restores the state saved by SetLocal.

Syntax

    ENDLOCAL

No parameters. Must be preceded by StartLocal.

ERASE or DEL

Protected and Real mode

Description

Deletes a file. Use RMDIR to delete directories.

Syntax

    ERASE File File File ... Option

File

Specify the file you want to delete; wildcards are permitted. You can specify this parameter more than once, so you delete several files with one command.

Option

/P   Prompts for confirmation before deleting a file.

/N   Suppresses the security prompt when you delete all the files of a
            directory.

EXIT

Protected and Real mode

Description

Exits the current command interpreter.

NOTE	You can only EXIT Real mode command interpreters if you didn't start with /P.

Syntax

```
Exit
```

EXTPROC

Protected mode

Description

Defines a new command interpreter.

Specify this command in the first line of a batch file. The rest of the batch file
will then be processed by a new command interpreter.

Syntax

```
EXTPROC File Parameter
```

File

Specifies the command interpreter. The parameters are passed to the command
interpreter.

FCBS

Real mode

Description

This command is used to specify the file-control-block (FCB) management for
DOS sessions.

This command is used in the CONFIG.SYS files.

Syntax

```
FCBS= Number1, Number2
```

Number1

Number1 The number of control blocks that can be open at the same time.

Number2

Number2 The number of files that can't be closed automatically if more than Number1 files are opened.

FDISK

Protected and Real mode

Description

Creates or deletes hard drive partition information. Use with extreme caution.

Syntax

```
FDISK

FDISK Parameter Options
```

Parameter

/QUERY Displays a list of partitions.

/CREATE

Creates the specified partition.

/DELETE

Deletes the specified partition.

/SETNAME

Sets the name for the specified partition.

/SETACCESS

Sets the specified partition as accessible.

/FILE:name

Executes the commands in the specified file.

Options

Options are used to limit FDISK actions.

/Name:name

Specifies a partition name.

/FSTYPE:x

Specifies a file system type.

/START:m
Specifies the partition starting location.

/SIZE:m Specifies the partition size.

/VTYPE:n
Specifies the partition type.

/BOOTABLE:s
Specifies the partition bootable status.

/BOOTMGR
Specifies a Boot Manager partition.

FDISKPM

Protected mode

Description

Used to create or delete hard drive partition information. Presentation Manager version of FDISK. Use with extreme caution.

Syntax

```
FDISKPM
```

FILES

Real mode

Description

This command specifies the number of files available for DOS sessions. It's used in the CONFIG.SYS files.

Syntax

```
FILE= Number
```

Number

Number   The number of files that can be opened.

FIND

Protected and Real mode

Description

Searches files for specified text.

Syntax

```
FIND Option "Text" File
```

Option

/V   Displays all lines that don't contain the text.

/C   Counts all lines containing the text. If you combine this parameter with /V, all lines that don't contain the text are counted. If you combine it with /N, /N will be ignored.

/I   Ignores case.

/N   Displays the line numbers of the lines found with the text.

Text

Specify the search text in quotation marks.

File

The file that's searched. Wildcards aren't permitted.

FOR

Protected and Real mode

Description

Executes a command several times.

In an OS/2 2.1 session you can redirect the output of a FOR loop to a file.

Syntax

```
FOR %%variable IN (condition) DO command
```

Var

This variable accepts the different values one after the other.

Condition

This condition is used to execute the loop.

Command

This command is executed.

FORMAT

Protected and Real mode

Description

Formats a diskette.

| **WARNING** | All the data on this diskette are deleted. |

Syntax

FORMAT Drive Option

Drive

The diskette in this drive is formatted.

Option

/Once   Formats only one diskette. The prompt that asks whether you want to format another diskette is suppressed.

/4   Formats a 360K diskette in a 1.2 Meg drive.

/T:xx   Specifies the number of tracks to be formatted.

/N:xx   Specifies the number of sectors to be created.

/F:xxx   Produces the specified format. Permissible values are 360, 720, 1200, 1440, and 2880.

/FS:xxx   Specifies the file system. The current values here are FAT and HPFS.

/L   Uses the long format procedure to format the IBM read/write optical drive.

/V:"Text"
           Specifies the name of the diskette.

FSACCESS

Real mode

Description

Used to assign drive letters in DOS sessions. Used to reassign drive letter when DOS is started from image files.

Syntax

FSACCESS ! Parameter

!

States that the following drive letter should not map OS/2 drives. Start with a colon.

Parameter

Specifies the drive letter to map. A minus sign specifies a range and an equal sign specifies an OS/2 drive.

FSFILTER

Real mode

Description

Used to provide access to OS/2 disk partitions from a DOS session. This device drive must be loaded in the CONFIG.SYS file.

Syntax

```
DEVICE=FSFILTER.SYS
```

This statement must be the first one in the CONFIG.SYS file.

GOTO

Protected and Real mode

Description

Jumps to a label in a batch file.

Syntax

```
GOTO Label
```

Label

Labels start with a colon.

GRAFTABL

Real mode

Description

Loads additional graphic characters into memory for DOS sessions. The command without any parameters displays the current code-page table.

Syntax

```
GRAFTABL Parameter
```

Parameter

nnn   Three digit number specifying code page.

?   Displays current code page number and a list of options.

/STA   Displays current code page number.

HELP

Protected and Real mode

Description

Displays a command description or an error message on the screen. This also switches off the status line.

Syntax

```
HELP Option
```

Option

On   Switches the status line on.

Off   Switches the status line off.

Text   Searches Help for the keyword text. You can specify the Help database in front of the keyword. The two current databases are REXX and CMDREF.

Number   Displays an explanation of the error message with the specified number. This number appears in front of each error message. They have the format SYSxxxx. You don't have to specify "Sys".

IF

Protected and Real mode

Description

Analyzes an Errorlevel and executes the appropriate command. In addition, this command checks whether a file exists.

Syntax

```
IF (NOT) Condition Command
```

Condition

If you specify a number here, it's compared with the return value of the last executed command.

The expression:

```
String1==String2
```

compares two texts with each other.

The expression:

```
Exist File
```

is true if the specified file exists.

You can place a NOT in front of all the conditions. This inverts the Boolean value.

Command

This command is executed if the condition is true.

IFS

Protected and Real mode

Description

Used to install file systems other than FAT systems. This device drive must be loaded in the CONFIG.SYS file.

Syntax

```
IFS=filename
```

This statement allows file systems to be installed. An example of an installable file system is the HPFS.IFS.

IOPL

Protected mode

Description

Used to allow input/output privileges to OS/2 processes. This must be loaded in the CONFIG.SYS file.

Syntax

```
IOPL= Parameter
```

Parameter

NN   Does not grant I/O privilege.

YES   Grants I/O privilege.

List   Lists the programs with I/O privilege.

JOIN

Real mode

Description

Makes a directory out of a drive. Any access to this directory is redirected to the drive.

If you specify the command without any parameters, then all current redirections are displayed.

Syntax

```
JOIN Drive Path Option
```

Drive

Enter the drive here.

Path

The drive is assigned to this path.

Option

/D   Cancels the assignment.

KEYB

Protected mode

Description

Sets a specific keyboard layout.

If you specify the command without any parameters, it displays the current status.

Syntax

```
KEYB Layout Subcountry
```

Layout

The following codes are permitted:

Codes	Country	Codes	Country
BE	Belgium	CF	Canada (French)
CS	Czechoslovakia	DK	Denmark
SU	Finland	FR	France
GR	Germany	HE	Hebrew

Codes	Country	Codes	Country
HU	Hungary	IS	Iceland
IT	Italy	LA	Latin America
NL	Netherlands	NO	Norway
PL	Poland	PO	Portugal
SP	Spain	SV	Sweden
SF	Switzerland (French)	SG	Switzerland (German)
TR	Turkey	UK	Great Britain
US	United States	YU	Yugoslavia

Subcountry

Some countries use more than one keyboard layout. Use the following codes to select them:

Codes	Country
243, 245	Czechoslovakia
189, 120	France
141, 142	Italy
166, 168	Great Britain

KEYS

Protected mode

Description

Turns the history buffer in the command line on and off.

Specify the command without parameters to display the current status.

To change the setting for all command interpreters in the CONFIG.SYS, assign the desired value to the KEYS environment variable.

Syntax

```
KEYS Option
```

Option

On   Switches the history buffer on.

Off   Switches the history buffer off.

List   Displays the contents of the history buffer.

LABEL

Protected and Real mode

Description

Use LABEL to create or change the names of hard drives or diskettes.

Specify the command without any parameters to display the name of the current drive.

Syntax

```
LABEL Drive Name
```

Drive

Specify the drive whose name you want to change here. If you don't specify a drive, the current drive is processed.

Name

Specify a name of up to 11 characters here.

If you don't specify a name here, you'll be prompted for one. If you just press Enter, the current name of the diskette/hard drive will be deleted.

LASTDRIVE

Real mode

Description

Used to specify last drive letter in DOS session. This must be loaded in the CONFIG.SYS file.

Syntax

```
LASTTDRIVE= Parameter
```

Parameter

Parameter   Last drive letter.

LIBPATH

Protected mode

Description

Used to specify path for OS/2 dynamic link libraries. This should be loaded in the CONFIG.SYS file.

Syntax

```
LIBPATH= Path
```

Path

Path   The path to search for OS/2 dynamic link libraries.

LH or LOADHIGH

Real mode

Description

Use LH or LOADHIGH to load TSR programs into Upper Memory Blocks (UMB) in a DOS Window.

To use LH or LOADHIGH, you must enter the following:

```
DOS = HIGH,UMB
```

in the CONFIG.SYS.

Syntax

```
LH File
LOADHIGH File
```

File

Specify the program you want to load into upper memory here. The filename can have a complete path.

MAKEINI

Protected mode

Description

If you can no longer read the OS2.INI file, use MAKEINI to create a new OS2.INI file.

NOTE To do this, start OS/2 from the first two installation diskettes and then press Esc to enter the OS/2 command line.

Delete the two files, OS2.INI and OS2SYS.INI, and start MAKEINI with the appropriate parameters. Then reboot the system.

Syntax

```
MAKEINI Target Source
```

Target

Specify the name of the target file or the target directory/drive here. Ordinarily you would specify OS2.INI or OS2SYS.INI.

Source

Specify the resource file here. Usually you would specify INI.RC or INISYS.RC.

MAXWAIT

Protected mode

Description

Used to set the amount of time a process waits before the system sets a new priority. This should be loaded in the CONFIG.SYS file.

Syntax

```
MAXWAIT= Num
```

Num

Num   Number of seconds to elapse before a change in priority. A value of 1 to 255 is acceptable.

MEM

Real mode

Description

Provides an overview of the free and allocated memory in DOS windows.

If you specify the command without any parameters, it displays an overview of the memory layout.

Syntax

```
MEM Option
```

Option

/P   Displays information about all the programs currently located in memory.

/D   Displays more information about all programs and drivers currently located in memory.

/C   Displays information on all programs located in conventional memory and in the Upper Memory Blocks (UMB).

MEMMAN

Protected mode

Description

Manages the memory allocation options for the OS/2 environment. This manages the swapping of memory segments from the disk into memory. This should be loaded in the CONFIG.SYS file.

Syntax

```
MAXWAIT= Parameters
```

Parameters

SWAP   Allows segment swapping.

NOSWAP   Does not allow segment swapping.

MOVE   Provides OS/2 1.3 compatibility.

NOMOVE   Provides OS/2 1.3 compatibility.

COMMIT   Commits storage on hard drive.

PROTECT   Enables some APIs to use protected memory.

MD or MKDIR

Protected and Real mode

Description

Use MD or MKDIR to create directories.

Syntax

```
MD Directory
MKDIR Directory
```

Directory

Specify the desired directory name here. You can specify more than one directory in Protected mode.

MODE

Protected and Real mode

Description

Use this command to set the operation mode for devices. In this case, devices are connected to the serial or parallel ports as well as the monitor and the disk drives.

Syntax

```
MODE Device Option
```

Device

You can use MODE to set four different kinds of devices.

COMn   Sets the parameters for the COMn ports.

CONn   Sets the parameters for the screen output.

LPTn   Sets the parameters for the LPTn ports.

DSKT   Sets the parameters for writing to diskettes.

COMn

Sets the parameters for the COMn ports. To make these settings, you must have already linked a "Base Asynchronous Communication Device Driver" in the CONFIG.SYS:

```
DEVICE = C:\OS2\COM.SYS
```

or

```
DEVICE = C:\OS2\COMDMA.SYS
```

Set the parameters for the COM ports as follows:

```
MODE COM1: baud, parity, databits, stopbits
```

CONn: Screen

On systems with more than one graphics card, you can set the video modes here.

Set the parameters for the screens as follows:

```
MODE CON1 CO80,43
```

This command switches the first screen to 80 character mode with 43 lines displayed.

LPTn: Printer

Make the settings for the parallel printer ports here.

Set the parameters for the printer ports in the following manner:

```
MODE LPT1 132,8
```

This command switches printer output to 132 character mode with 8 lines per inch.

DSKT: Diskettes

Use this parameter to set the parameters for writing to diskettes.

Set the parameters for write verification on diskettes in the following manner:

```
MODE DSKT VER=ON
```

This command switches on write verification on diskettes. By default, this option is off. If you switch this option on, accesses to diskettes will slow down.

MORE

Protected and Real mode

Description

This routine reads data from the default input device and then outputs this data on the default output device. As soon as the screen page is full, output stops.

Normally MORE is used by using an input/output redirection:

```
MORE <LONGER.TXT
```

The other option is to use a pipe:

```
DIR C:\ /S | MORE
```

Syntax

```
MORE
```

MOVE

Protected and Real mode

Description

Use the MOVE command to move a file or an entire group of files from one directory to another.

Syntax

```
MOVE File Target
```

File

Specify the files you want to move here. The filename can include a complete path. You can also use wildcards.

Target

Specify the target directory here.

PATCH

Protected and Real mode

Description

Use the PATCH command to correct and optimize your IBM software.

Occasionally IBM performs error correction and optimizations on all programs. When IBM does this, you don't have to pay a lot of money for a 2.1a version, which is called an update. Instead, you can use CSD (Corrective Service Disk) diskettes, which have "automatic patches".

You can copy these CSD diskettes at no extra charge at IBM dealers or download them from many BBSs. This ensures that your software is always current.

So if you ever discover an error, report it to IBM.

Syntax

```
PATCH File Option
```

File

Specify the PATCH file of the CSD diskette here. The filename can include a complete path.

Option

/A   Switches to automatic patch mode.

PATH

Protected and Real mode

Description

Use PATH to set the search path for commands and programs.

Specify the command without any parameters to display the current search path.

Syntax

```
PATH Path
```

Path

Always specify the complete search path here.

PAUSE

Protected and Real mode

Description

Interrupts a batch file until the user presses a key.

Syntax

```
PAUSE Comment
```

Comment

If you don't specify a comment, the following message appears with PAUSE:

```
Press any key when ready...
```

You could also precede this message with one of your own:

```
PAUSE Press the spacebar to continue...
```

The comment makes the PAUSE command more flexible.

PAUSEONERROR

Protected and Real mode

Description

Stops or allows the display of error message during the CONFIG.SYS processing.

Syntax

```
PAUSE YES/NO
```

YES/NO

YES allows the system to pause, NO does not.

PICVIEW

Protected mode

Description

Load the PICVIEW program to display an image file on the screen.

Syntax

```
PICVIEW File Option
```

File

Specify the filename here. The filename can include a complete path.

Option

/MET The picture is a special meta file. You can exchange these files between different applications.

/PIF The picture is in PIF (Picture Interchange File) format.

/P   The picture is output on the printer.

/S   PICVIEW returns to the default values of the window position after displaying the picture.

PMREXX

Protected mode

Description

Use this command to start a REXX interpreter under the Presentation Manager. All output is then redirected to a window.

The REXTRY.CMD file will give you an input line for entering single REXX instructions.

Syntax

```
PMREXX File
```

File

Specify a REXX file (*.CMD) here. You can include a complete path in the filename.

PRINT

Protected and Real mode

Description

Use this command to print files or groups of files.

Syntax

```
PRINT Option1 File Option2
```

Option1

/B   Place a /B in front of the filename to eliminate end of file characters. For example, this is useful when printing listings.

/D:Device

Specify a printer port here. This is the port where the program will print. You could specify PRN, LPT1, LPT2, and LPT3.

If you're working in a network, you can also specify LPT4 to LPT9.

File

Specify the file you want to print here. You can include a complete path in the filename. You can also use wildcards.

Option2

/C   Protected mode only:
            Stops current printout, then prints the next file.

/T   Protected mode only:
            Stops all printouts. None of the files in the print queue will be printed.

PRINTMONBUFSIZE

Protected and Real mode

Description

Specifies the size of the parallel port buffer. Use this command in the CONFIG.SYS file.

Syntax

```
PRINTMONBUFSIZE Num1, Num2, Num3
```

Num1-3

Numx   Specifies the LPT port.

PRIORITY

Protected and Real mode

Description

Specifies the priority calculation in regular threads. Use this command in the CONFIG.SYS file.

Syntax

```
PRIORITY  Parameter
```

Parameter

DYNAMIC   Allows dynamic calculation of threads.

ABSOLUTE   Allows absolute calculation of threads.

PRIORITY_DISK_IO

Protected and Real mode

Description

Specifies disk input/output priority for applications. Use this command in the CONFIG.SYS file.

Syntax

```
PRIORITY_DISK_IO   YES/NO
```

YES/NO

YES   Gives priority to application running in foreground.

NO   All applications have the same priority.

PROMPT

Protected and Real mode

Description

Use the PROMPT command to change the prompt.

Specify the command without any parameters to set the default prompt.

Syntax

```
PROMPT Text
```

Text

This is where you enter the text you want to appear after the prompt.

The following codes are possible:

Code	Prompt Display	Code	Prompt Display
$B	Pipe symbol (l)	$D	Date
$E	Escape character	$G	> character
$H	Deletes left character	$L	< character
$N	Current drive	$P	Current subdirectory
$Q	= sign	$T	Time
$V	OS/2 version number	$_	New line
$$	$ sign		

PROTECTONLY

Protected mode

Description

Allows memory below 640K to be used by OS/2 programs. Use this command in the CONFIG.SYS file.

Syntax

```
PROTECTONLY   YES/NO
```

YES/NO

YES   Allows memory below 640K to be used by OS/2 programs.

NO   Allows program to be run in DOS sessions.

PROTSHELL

Protected mode

Description

Loads user interface and OS/2 CMD.EXE command processor. Use this command in the CONFIG.SYS file.

Syntax

```
PROTSHELL  = Filename
```

Filename

User interface and command processor file name.

PSTAT

Protected mode

Description

Use this utility program to display internal system information. Usually only software developers need this information.

The program displays processes, threads, system semaphores, memory information, and information about dynamic link libraries.

Specify the command without parameters to display the current system status.

Syntax

```
PSTAT Option
```

Option

/C   Displays all running processes and threads.

/S   Displays detailed information about the individual threads.

/L   Displays the dynamic link libraries for the processes.

/M   Displays all information shared by the processes.

/P:pid Displays special information about the specified process.

RECOVER

Protected and Real mode

Description

Use the RECOVER command to recover files, directories, or entire hard drives, in case defective sectors occur.

However, use this command carefully. Inappropriate or unnecessary use of RECOVER causes data loss. All files will be renamed and restructured.

Syntax

```
RECOVER File
```

File

Specify the name of the file you want to recover here. The filename can include a complete path.

You could also specify a drive instead of a filename here, for example, to restore a diskette. Use this option carefully, since all files will be renamed and restructured.

REM

Protected and Real mode

Description

Used to add comment lines in the CONFIG.SYS file.

Syntax

```
REM Comment
```

Commented

Comment line that will be displayed unless ECHO is OFF.

REN or RENAME

Protected and Real mode

Description

Use REN or RENAME to rename files or entire groups of files in a directory.

Syntax

```
REN File File
RENAME File File
```

File

The first parameter represents the file or group of files you want to rename. The second parameter specifies the new name.

You can use wildcards in both cases.

REPLACE

Protected and Real mode

Description

Use the REPLACE command to replace files in a directory. When you use this command, files that have the same name are completely overwritten. REPLACE copies any files that aren't in the target directory yet to this directory.

Syntax

```
REPLACE File Directory Option
```

File

Specify the files to be replaced here. You can include a complete path in the filename. You can also use wildcards.

Directory

Specify the directory name here, in which the files are to be replaced.

Option

/A	Copies only files that aren't in the target directory yet.
/S	Copies only files that are already in the target directory.
/P	Displays the name of every file before it is copied. This lets you decide whether you want to copy the file.
/R	Overwrites read-only files in the target directory.
/W	This parameter is useful for batch files. REPLACE waits for the user to press a key before replacing, which gives you time to insert a diskette.

/U   Only overwrites files that are older than the source files.

/F   REPLACE aborts the copying process in cases where the file system of
          the target drive doesn't support extended attributes, and one of the
          files to be copied has extended attributes.

RESTORE

Protected mode

Description

Use this command to restore files from a previous backup.

Syntax

`RESTORE Source Target Option`

Source

Specify the source drive for the backup here.

Target

Specify the target drive (i.e., the drive to which you want to copy the backup
files).

Option

/P   Before the files are restored, you're prompted to save read-only files,
          hidden files, or files that have been changed since the last backup.

/M   Restores only files that have been changed since the last backup.

/B:mm-dd-yy
          Restores only files that have been changed on or before the specified
          date.

/A:mm-dd-yy
          Restores only files that have been changed on or after the specified
          date.

/E:hh:mm:ss
          Restores only files that have been changed on or before the specified
          time.

/L:hh:mm:ss
          Restores only files that have been changed on or after the specified
          time.

/S   Also restores all files in subdirectories.

/N   Restores only files that aren't present on the target drive.

/F   If the file system of the target drive doesn't support extended
          attributes, but one of the files contains extended attributes, RESTORE
          aborts the copying process.

/D   Displays a list of all the files of the backup. You must also specify a
          target drive here, even though you aren't restoring the backup.

RD or RMDIR

Protected and Real mode

Description

Use RD or RMDIR to delete empty directories.

Syntax

```
RD Directory
RMDIR Directory
```

Directory

Specify the directory you want to delete here. It has the same structure as a
normal path.

You can even specify more than one directory in Protected mode.

RMSIZE

Real mode

Description

Allows you to set the highest address accessible by the DOS environment. Use
this command in the CONFIG.SYS file.

Syntax

```
RMSIZE   Num
```

Num

The number, between 0 and 640 that represents 1024 bytes, that sets the highest
DOS memory setting.

RUN

Real mode

Description

Runs a system program during system initialization. Use this command in the
CONFIG.SYS file, but all DEVICE commands will be processed first.

Syntax

```
RUN  Filename
```

Filename

Name of the file to run.

SET

Protected and Real mode

Description

Use SET to assign values to environment variables.

If you specify the command without any parameters, it displays the current contents of all the variables.

You can also use SET to set variables in the OS/2 CONFIG.SYS.

Syntax

```
SET String= String
```

String

The first string specifies the name of the system variable. The second string is the value, or the string to be assigned to the system variable.

To assign the value "secured" to the DATA variable, enter:

```
SET DATA=secured
```

Don't use the following characters in strings: = : < > |.

SETBOOT

Protected mode

Description

Use the SETBOOT command to set the parameters for the Boot Manager (provided there is one; refer to Chapter 1 on Dual Boot Installation) from the command line.

Syntax

```
SETBOOT Option
```

Option

/T:x   Use this option to set the "Timeout" value. This is the number of seconds after which the default partition is started.

/T:NO   Switches off the "Timeout" starter.

/M:m   Sets the mode for the Boot Manager. "n" represents Normal mode.

However, if you specify an "a" here, the command switches to Extended mode, in which additional information is displayed.

/Q   Use this option to determine the current settings of the Boot Manager.

/B   Use this parameter to produce a regular shutdown. The computer then reboots.

/X;x   Sets startup index (x, 0-3) which indicates partition to boot.

/N:name Sets startup name which indicates operating system to boot.

SETLOCAL

Protected mode

Description

The values of the environment variables are saved and can then be changed locally in a batch file.

The opposite of this command is ENDLOCAL, which restores the original status.

Syntax

```
SETLOCAL
```

To use a new search path only within a batch file, use the following structure:

```
.
.
.
SETLOCAL
A:
CD \ELSEWHER
PATH A:\;A:\ELSEWHER
.
.
.
ENDLOCAL
```

After this batch file finishes, all the environment variables possess their original values.

SHELL

Real mode

Description

Loads DOS command processor, COMMAND.EXE. Use this command in the CONFIG.SYS file.

Syntax

```
SHELL  = Filename
```

Filename

Command processor file name, if omitted default command processor is loaded.

SHIFT

Protected and Real mode

Description

SHIFT lets you use more than 10 parameters in batch files.

Syntax

```
SHIFT
```

You can use parameters %0 to %9 in batch files. If the parameters have the following contents:

```
%0 = '0'
%1 = '1'
%2 = '2'
```

%3 - %9 are empty.

By calling SHIFT once, you get the following contents:

```
%0 = '1'
%1 = '2'
```

%2 - %9 are empty.

SORT

Protected and Real mode

Description

This sorting routine reads data from the default input device, sorts the data and then outputs the data on the default output device.

The maximum size of a sorted file is about 63K.

Usually you sort by using an input/output redirection twice:

```
SORT <Unsorted.Data >Sorted.Data
```

Syntax

```
SORT Option
```

Option

/R   Sorts backwards (in reverse), from "Z" to "A".

/+n   Specifies that the sorting take place after the "n"th column. Usually
          sorting starts at the beginning of the line.

SPOOL

Protected mode

Description

Use SPOOL to specify the port for the printer output.

Specify the command without any parameters to display the current status.

Syntax

```
SPOOL Option
```

Option

/D:Device
          Specifies the input device. Your application prints to this device.
          Possible input devices are PRN, LPT1, LPT2, LPT3.

/O:Device
          Specifies the output device. The data are output to this device.
          Possible output devices are PRN, LPT1, LPT2, LPT3 as well as COM1 to
          COM4.

/Q   Displays a list of the current output redirections.

START

Protected mode

Description

Use START to start another CMD.EXE command processor. This command
processor then appears in the Window List (Task Manager, Ctrl + Esc).

Usually, you use START to start programs during system startup. To do this,
create a STARTUP.CMD file, in which your programs start in sequence with the
help of the START command.

If you specify the command without any parameters, it only starts another CMD.EXE.

Syntax

```
START "Title" Option Command (Commands-)Parameter
```

"Title"

Specify the name of the program, in quotation marks, that you want to appear later in the Window List (Task Manager, [Ctrl] + [Esc]).

This title can contain up to 60 characters.

Option

There are six groups of commands:

With or without CMD.EXE

/K   CMD.EXE starts before the actual command and the command processor remains after the command is finished.

/C   CMD.EXE starts before the actual command, but the command processor terminates after the command is finished.

/N   CMD.EXE doesn't start before the actual command. You cannot use batch files or internal commands (such as COPY) here.

Start in the foreground or background

/B   Starts a process in the background. This is the default setting.

/F   Starts a process in the foreground. If you specify one of the following parameters, /FS, /WIN, or /PM, then the process automatically starts in the foreground.

Title and Program Names

/PGM   If you specify /PGM, then the title of the program is also used as the actual program name.

Full-screen or Window mode

/FS   Specifies that the program is a full-screen application, which must be started in a session that's independent from the Workplace Shell.

/WIN   Specifies that the program is an OS/2 or DOS application that should run in a window.

/PM   Use this option to specify that the program is a Presentation Manager application.

/DOS   Use this parameter to start a program as a DOS application. This is useful for Family API (FAPI) applications. If you specify the parameter, you start a DOS box.

Window size

/MAX   Starts the application in a maximized window. This parameter doesn't affect full-screen applications.

/MIN   Starts the application in a minimized window as an icon. This parameter doesn't affect full-screen applications.

Using the environment memory

/I   Usually in a session produced by START, the values are taken from the current environment.

To obtain precisely defined initial states, specify /I. This reinitializes the environment of the new session from the CONFIG.SYS.

SUBST

Real mode

Description

Use SUBST to assign a drive letter to a directory. This is helpful for extremely long directory names.

Specify the command without any parameters to display all the current assignments.

Syntax

```
SUBST Drive Path Option
```

Drive

Specify the drive letter by which you want to address the path. Make sure that this drive hasn't been used yet and that the:

```
LASTDRIVE = Z
```

entry in the CONFIG.SYS is set high enough.

Path

Specify the path that you want to replace.

Option

/D   If you specify a drive letter here instead of a path, the assignment will be canceled.

SWAPPATH

Real mode

Description

Use SWAPPATH to specify the size and location of the swap file. The swap file stores memory segments on disk when more memory is required.

Syntax

```
SWAPPATH Drive Minfree Initial
```

Drive

Specify the drive letter and path where the swap file should be stored.

Minfree

Specify the free space to be left on the disk.

Initial

Specify the initial size of the swap file.

SYSLEVEL

Protected mode

Description

Specifies the version number of the kernel.

Use this version number to determine the CSD level at which you're working. CSD is an abbreviation for "Corrective Service Disk".

When appropriate, IBM performs error correction and optimizations on all programs. When IBM does this, you don't have to pay a lot of money for a 2.1a version, which is called an update. Instead, you can use CSD diskettes, which contain "automatic patches".

You can get these CSD diskettes at IBM dealers and download them from many BBSs. This ensures that your software is always current.

So if you ever discover an error, report it to IBM.

Syntax

```
SYSLEVEL
```

You see a screen display similar to the following:

```
C:\OS2\INSTALL\SYSLEVEL.OS2
IBM OS/2 Base Operating System
Version 2.1    Component ID 000000000
Current CSD level: XR00000
Prior   CSD level: XR00000
```

SYSLOG

Protected mode

Description

Use this to output a formatted screen display or printout of the system error log.

To be able to use SYSLOG, you must add the following lines to the CONFIG.SYS:

```
DEVICE = C:\OS2\LOG.SYS
```

and

```
RUN = \OS2\SYSTEM\LOGDAEM.EXE
```

Syntax

```
SYSLOG Option
```

Option

/S   Switches off the error log temporarily.

/R   Switches on the error log.

/P:Filename
          Use this option to redirect the information about the errors to another file. You can include a complete path with the filename.

/W:x   Use this to set the maximum size of the error log. By default, the file is 64K, the minimum is 4K.

THREADS

Protected mode

Description

Sets the maximum number of threads, or independent action for OS/2.

Specify the command without any parameters to display the current time.

Syntax

```
THREADS = Number
```

Number

The number of independent threads.

TIME

Protected and Real mode

Description

Use this command to set the internal system clock.

Specify the command without any parameters to display the current time.

Syntax

```
TIME Time
```

Time

Specify the time as a parameter.

TIMESLICE

Protected mode

Description

Sets the amount of processor time allocated to DOS and OS/2 programs. Use this command in the CONFIG.SYS file.

Syntax

```
TIMESLICE  Parameters
```

Parameters

x   Minimum timeslice value in milliseconds, greater than or equal to 32.

y   Maximum timeslice value in milliseconds, greater than or equal to the minimum value and less than 65536 sypl.

TRACE

Protected mode

Description

TRACE is important for software developers and for technical support. If the TRACE function is switched on, all system calls are included in the log.

To do this, add the following line to the CONFIG.SYS:

```
TRACE=ON
```

Syntax

```
TRACE Option
```

Option

ON   Switches TRACE mode on.

OFF   Switches TRACE mode off.

TRACEBUF

Protected mode

Description

TRACEBUF sets the size of the TRACE buffer. Use this command in the
CONFIG.SYS file.

Syntax

```
TRACE = Num
```

Num

Num   Number, from 1 to 63, representing size of trace buffer in multiple of
            1024 bytes.

TRACEFMT

Protected mode

Description

TRACEFMT is also important for software developers and for technical support.
If the TRACE function is switched on, all system calls are included in the log.
You can use TRACEFMT to display this file on the screen or print it on the
printer.

Syntax

```
TRACEFMT Filename
```

File

Specify the TRACE file here. You can include a complete path in the filename.

TREE

Protected and Real mode

Description

Displays the complete directory structure of a drive. You can also have it include
all files in the display.

Specify the command without parameters to display the directory tree of the
current drive.

Syntax

```
TREE Drive Option
```

Drive

Specify the drive whose directory structure you want to display.

Option

/F   Includes files in the display.

TYPE

Protected and Real mode

Description

Displays the contents of a file on the screen. You can specify more than one file in Protected mode.

Syntax

```
TYPE Filename
```

File

Specify the file you want to display. You can include a complete path in the filename.

To print a file, redirect the output to the printer:

```
TYPE INFOS.TXT >PRN
```

UNDELETE

Protected and Real mode

Description

In most cases, this command is able to restore files that have been accidentally deleted.

Set the DELDIR environment variable in the CONFIG.SYS in the following manner:

```
SET DELDIR = Drive:\Path, Number; Drive2:\...
```

Syntax

```
UNDELETE Filename
```

File

Specify the file you want to recover here. You can include a complete path in the filename.

Option

/A   Recovers all files that are still intact. There isn't a prompt in between
          files.

/F   Overwrites the files so that they cannot be recovered.

/L   Displays a list of all recoverable files.

/S   Indicates that subdirectories should also be checked.

UNPACK

Protected and Real mode

Description

Unpacks compressed files from the OS/2 2.1 Installation diskettes. These files
have an "@" as the last character in the filename.

Syntax

UNPACK File Path Option

File

Specify the file you want unpacked here. You can include a complete path with
the filename.

Path

Specify the target path for the file here. It matches the structure of the normal
path. This is where the file is unpacked.

Option

/V   Specifies whether data should be verified after being written to a
          diskette/hard drive. Set /V to switch on verification.

/F   Protected mode only:
          If the file system of the target drive doesn't support extended
          attributes, but a file contains extended attributes, UNPACK aborts the
          unpacking process.

/N:Filename
          Specify a special file under Filename. This is the only file that the
          command will unpack.

/SHOW
          Displays all available target paths and filenames in the package.

VER

Protected and Real mode

Description

Displays the OS/2 version number.

Syntax

```
VER
```

In both Protected and Real mode, you'll see the line:

```
The Operating System/2 Version is 2.1
```

VERIFY

Protected and Real mode

Description

Specifies whether data should be verified after it's written to a diskette/hard drive.

Specify the command without any parameters to display the current status.

Syntax

```
VERIFY Option
```

Option

ON   Switches verification on.

OFF   Switches verification off.

By default, VERIFY is switched off.

VIEW

Protected mode

Description

VIEW displays the on-line documents (*.INF) that were produced by the "Information Presentation Facility" (IPF) compiler.

Syntax

```
VIEW File Topic
```

File

Specify the INF file here. You can include a complete path with the filename.

Topic

VIEW searches for information about the specified topic.

VMDISK

Real mode

Description

Use VMDISK to create an image file of a DOS boot diskette. Then you could, for example, boot a DOS window from this image file.

Syntax

```
VMDISK Source Target Option
```

Source

Specify in which drive the boot diskette, from which you want to make an image file, is located.

Target

Specify the name of the target file and, if necessary, the target directory/drive.

The following preparations are necessary in order to use such a boot diskette properly:

Enter the following line as the first line in the CONFIG.SYS:

```
DEVICE = FSFILTER.SYS
```

Now copy:

```
C:\OS2\MDOS\FSFILTER.SYS
```

to the root directory of the boot diskette.

If XMS (HIMEM.SYS) or EMS (EMM386.SYS) drivers are present, replace them with:

```
DEVICE = C:\OS2\MDOS\HIMEM.SYS
DEVICE = C:\OS2\MDOS\EMM386.SYS
```

OS/2 2.1 provides mouse support. If you still require a mouse driver, add:

```
C:\OS2\MDOS\MOUSE
```

to the AUTOEXEC.BAT.

VOL

Protected and Real mode

Description

VOL displays the name of diskettes and hard drives. Beginning with DOS 4.0, the serial number is also displayed.

Specify the command without any parameters to display the name of the current drive.

Syntax

```
VOL Drive
```

Drive

Specify the drive containing the diskette/hard drive whose name you want to display.

You can also specify more than one drive at the same time in Protected mode.

XCOPY

Protected and Real mode

Description

XCOPY (="eXtended COPY") is an extension of the normal COPY command. Use XCOPY to copy entire files, directories, or directory trees. You can also process file attributes.

Syntax

```
XCOPY Source Target Option
```

Source

Specify the file you want copied here. You can include a complete path with the filename. Instead of specifying a file, you can also use wildcards, entire directories, or a complete drive.

Target

Specify the name of the target file, directory, or drive. If the target directory doesn't exist yet, it's created.

Option

/A   Copies only files that have been changed since the last copy (with BACKUP or XCOPY) (in other words, files with a set archive bit). The archive bit isn't cleared.

/D:dd-mm-yy
Copies only files whose creation date is more recent or the same as the specified date. The date format corresponds to the one set in the CONFIG.SYS (COUNTRY command).

/E   Empty subdirectories are included in the copy. Combine this option with /S to copy the entire directory structure.

/F   Protected mode only:
If the file system of the target drive doesn't support any extended attributes, but a file contains these attributes, XCOPY aborts the copying process.

/M   Copies only files that have been changed since the last copy (with BACKUP or XCOPY) (with set archive bit). However, unlike /A, the archive bit is cleared.

/P   For each file, you must confirm a prompt before it's copied.

/S   Copies all subdirectories containing files.

/V   Each copied file is verified.

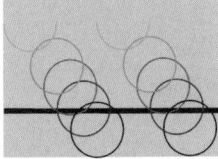

Stepping Up To OS/2 2.1

——— Index ———

A

Activities list (PM Diary)..............................142
Alarms (PM Diary)...............................142-143
Autocheck:
HPFS drives..47

B

Batch files..175-179
CMD extension...175
Blocks
Using in PM Chart...................................165
Using in the Icon Editor.......................150
Using in the System Editor..................154
Using with the Enhanced Editor.........157
Boot Manager...16-18

C

Cache:
HPFS...46-48
Calendar (PM Diary)........................143-144
Calculator (PM Diary)................................143
Cat and Mouse...172
Changing partitions
In Drive windows...................................70-71
Chess..171
Color settings..131
Colors:
Using in the Icon Editor.........................152
Using in the System Editor...................156
Command line...88
Help...89-90
Prompts...88
Status line...89
Command Reference......................................94
Finding commands....................................94
Also see OS/2 2.1 commands
Complete installation...................................23

CONFIG.SYS:
Changing...40
CUA (Common User Access)......................51

D

Daily Planner (PM Diary)...........................144
Data object..83
Database (PM Diary)...................................145
DDE...124-125
Desktop settings.......................................82-83
Device drivers:
DOS Windows...115
Diagram:
Creating in PM Chart..............................166
Directory window settings.....................78-81
Diskettes:
Changing sort sequence...........................69
Checking..68-69
Formatting...67-68
Display setup...37
DOS (MS-DOS):
Migrating applications.......................38-40
Launching from OS/2.................................99
Setting up DOS programs.....................100
Settings for DOS programs..........100-111
DOS Window:
Booting..113
DOS windows:
Device drivers...115
Memory management..............................111
Drive windows...65-71
Changing partitions.............................70-71
Changing sort sequence......................69-70
Checking diskettes...............................68-69
Formatting diskettes............................67-68
Free disk space..70
Opening...65-66
Searching for files................................66-67
Dynamic Data Exchange...................124-125

E

ENDLOCAL...175
Enhanced Editor..................................156-162
        Default settings.............................160-161
        Editor commands............................161-162
        Using..157-160
Extended attributes (HPFS)....................44-46

F

FDISK.....................................6, 11-12, 70-71
File swapping...................................121-125
File systems..7-9
        File Allocation Table...............................7
        HPFS..7-9
        installing..17-18
Filenames
        HPFS..42-43

G

Games...171-173
        Cat and Mouse.......................................172
        Chess...171
        Jigsaw..172
        Klondike..173
        Reversi...173
        Scramble...172

H

Hard drive:
        Partitioning..11-12
Help:
        Command Reference............................94-96
        From the command line....................89-90
        Glossary..98
        Help system...91-98
        Master Help Index...............................97-98
        REXX Information..................................96-97
        Start Here..92-93
        Tutorial...92
HPFS..41-50
        Advantages..7-9
        Autocheck..47
        Caching..46-48
        Compatibility..41-42
        Extended attributes..............................44-46
        Filenames...42-43
        Lazy Write...47
        Operation..48-50

I

Icon Editor..148-153
        Additional functions............................153
        Changing colors......................................152
        Creating a new icon..............................153
        Options..151
        Using...148
Icon View...66
Image file..114
Installation..1-40
        Backup hard drive.................................2-3
        Backup original diskettes.......................1
        Basic installation....................................6-7
        CD-ROM Device Support......................25
        Changing CONFIG.SYS.........................40
        Changing partitions.............................6-9
        Complete installation......................22-23
        Country..25
        Display setup..37
        DOS and OS/2 together.............................9
        Dual boot method.................................4-6
        File systems...7-9
        Keyboard..25
        Methods...4-7
        Minimal installation........................22-23
        Mouse...24
        OS/2 with DOS......................................18-21
        Port setting..27
        Preparation..1
        Primary display...24
        Printer setup..37-38
        Printer support...26
        Requirements...3-4
        SCSI Adapter Support...............................26
        Secondary display.....................................25
        Selective installation.........................22-27
        Serial Device Support...............................24
        Starting...10-12
        System configuration........................24-27
        VGA cards with autodetect........................9
        VGA cards with IRQ2..................................9

J

Jigsaw...172

K

Keyboard settings.....................................134
Klondike...173

L

Launching Windows programs 118
Lazy Write (HPFS) 47

M

Master Help Index 97
Migrating applications 38-40
Minimal installation 22-23
Minimized Window Viewer 74
Monthly Planner (PM Diary) 145
Mouse:
    Configuring 125
    Mouse settings 125
Multitasking 121-124

N

Note Pad (PM Diary) 145

O

Objects:
    Associations 88
    Copying and moving objects 60-61
    Creating new objects 84-88
    Deleting objects 61-62
    Opening an object 59-60
    Printing objects 62
    Selecting objects 60
    Shadow objects 62-64
    Also see **Workplace Shell**
Original submenu 62
OS/2:
    Creating partitions 12-18
    Deleting from hard drive 21
    Installation 1-40
    Installing with DOS 5-6
    Command reference 183-253
    See also specific topic
OS/2 2.1 commands:
    ANSI 186
    APPEND 187
    ASSIGN 187
    ATTRIB 188
    AUTOFAIL 189
    BACKUP 189
    BASEDEV 191
    BOOT 191
    BREAK 191
    BUFFERS 192
    CACHE 192

CALL 192
CHCP 193
CD or CHDIR 193
CHKDSK 194
CLS 195
CMD 195
CODEPAGE 196
COMMAND 196
COMP 197
COPY 197
COUNTRY 199
CREATEDD 200
DATE 200
DDINSTALL 201
DEBUG 201
DEL 203
DETACH 203
DEVICE 203
DEVICEHIGH 204
DEVINFO 204
DIR 204
DISKCACHE 206
DISKCOMP 206
DISKCOPY 207
DOSKEY 207
DOS 208
DPATH 208
EAUTIL 209
ECHO 210
ENDLOCAL 210
ERASE or DEL 210
EXIT 211
EXTPROC 211
FCBS 211
FDISK 212
FDISKPM 213
FILES 213
FIND 213
FOR 214
FORMAT 215
FSACCESS 215
FSFILTER 216
GOTO 216
GRAFTABL 216
HELP 217
IF 217
IFS 218
IOPL 218
JOIN 219
KEYB 219
KEYS 220
LABEL 221
LASTDRIVE 221
LIBPATH 221
LH or LOADHIGH 222
MAKEINI 222
MAXWAIT 223

MEM..223
MEMMAN.....................................224
MD or MKDIR.............................224
MODE..224
MORE...226
MOVE...226
PATCH..227
PATH...227
PAUSE...228
PAUSEONERROR.......................228
PICVIEW......................................228
PMREXX......................................229
PRINT...229
PRINTMONBUFSIZE.................230
PRIORITY....................................230
PRIORITY_DISK_IO 231
PROMPT......................................231
PROTECTONLY.........................232
PROTSHELL.................................232
PSTAT...232
RECOVER....................................233
REM...233
REN or RENAME.......................234
REPLACE......................................234
RESTORE......................................235
RD or RMDIR............................236
RMSIZE...236
RUN...236
SET...237
SETBOOT....................................237
SETLOCAL..................................238
SHELL...239
SHIFT..239
SORT..239
SPOOL..240
START...240
SUBST...242
SWAPPATH.................................243
SYSLEVEL....................................243
SYSLOG.......................................244
THREADS....................................244
TIME..245
TIMESLICE..................................245
TRACE..245
TRACEBUF..................................246
TRACEFMT..................................246
TREE...246
TYPE...247
UNDELETE.................................247
UNPACK......................................248
VER..249
VERIFY...249
VIEW...249
VMDISK.......................................250
VOL..251
XCOPY...251

P

Partition editor:
   See FDISK
Partitions:
   Access..13
   Boot Manager...........................16
   Changing..................................6-9
   Creating...........................12, 15-16
   FS type..................................14-15
   Megabytes................................15
   Naming......................................12
   Status...................................13-14
Planner Archive (PM Diary).....................146
PM Chart......................................162-167
   Additional settings..............166-167
   Block operations.................165-166
   Creating a diagram................166
   Tool Bar.............................163-165
PM Diary..141-148
   Activities List..........................142
   Alarms......................................142
   Calculator.................................143
   Calendar....................................144
   Daily Planner...........................144
   Database...................................145
   Monthly Planner......................145
   Note Pad...................................145
   Planner Archive.......................146
   Spreadsheet..............................146
   Sticky Pad.................................147
   To Do List Archive..................148
   To Do list..................................148
   Tune Editor...............................148
PM Terminal.................................167-168
Printer icon..56
Printer installation............................137
Printer setup.................................37-38
Printing
   From DOS Windows and Windows.139
   Hardcopies..........................139-140
   Installation.........................137-138
   Spooler................................138-139
   Under OS/2.............................137
Productivity folder.....................141-170
   Enhanced Editor.................156-162
   Icon Editor..........................148-153
   PM Chart..............................162-166
   PM Diary..............................141-148
   PM Terminal............................167
   Pulse...168
   Seek and Scan Files.................168
   System Editor.......................153-156
Program groups.............................71-73

Programs:
Launching..122
Pulse...168

R

Replacing text:
Enhanced editor..........................158
System Editor...............................155
Reversi...173
REXX..175-179
Basic information................................176
Launching programs.............................179
Writing programs...................................176
REXX Information...96
Rubberbanding:
Selecting objects......................56-57, 60

S

Scramble..172
Searching for files....................................169
Searching for text:
Enhanced Editor.......................158
System Editor...............................155
Seek and Scan Files.........................168-170
Options...170
Working with the list............................170
Selective installation.........................23-24
Setup..27
SETLOCAL...175
Setting an alarm:
PM Diary..142
Settings...73-83, 90
Data object...83
Desktop settings.............................82-83
Directory window settings.................78-81
General settings....................................75
Program settings...............................75-78
Window settings...............................74-75
Windows programs..............................119
Shadow objects....................................62-64
Creating..63-64
Shadows...64
Shredder icon.................................55, 61, 83
Shut down..59
Sound:
Setting...126
Spooler..138
Spreadsheet (PM Diary).......................146
Status line..89
Sticky Pad..147
System clock..135

System Editor.................................153-156
Block operations...........................154-155
Color..156
Search and Replace.......................155-156
System Setup..................................125-136
Clock..135
Colors...131
Country...130
Fonts..131
Keyboard..134
Mouse..125
Sound..126
Spooler..133
System...127
WIN-OS/2 Setup programs................136

T

Templates...84-88
Associations...88
Creating Templates............................85-88
Deleting Templates..................................88
Templates folder......................................84
Using Templates...................................84-85
To Do list (PM Diary)............................148
To Do List Archive (PM Diary).................148
Tool bar (PM Chart)................................163
Tune Editor (PM Diary)............................148

U

UNDELETE..62

V

VGA cards:
IRQ2 considerations......................................9
OS/2 Installation considerations............9

W

BOARD..119
Windows:
Device drivers......................................120
Windows applications:
Migrating...38-40
Windows programs..........................117-120
Launching..118
Setting up...118
Settings...119, 136
Using in OS/2......................................117
WIN_RUNMODE.....................................119
WIN_DDE...119

WIN_CLIPBOARD 119
Workplace Shell 51-90
     Command Line 88
     Copying objects 60-61
     Deleting objects 61-62
     Drive Windows 65-71
     Moving objects 60-61
     Object Menu 53-55
     Opening objects 59-60
     Printer icon 56
     Printing 62
     Renaming objects 64
     Rubberbanding 56-57
     Selecting objects 60
     Setting up 55-59
     Settings 73-83, 90
     Shadow objects 62-64
     Shredder 55, 61, 83-84
     Shut down 59
     Startup Screen 52-53
     Templates 84-88
     Veto symbol 55
     Working with Objects 59-65
     Workplace Shell objects 53-64

Abacus

pc catalog

Order Toll Free 1-800-451-4319

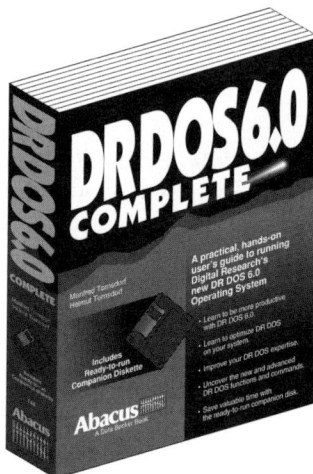

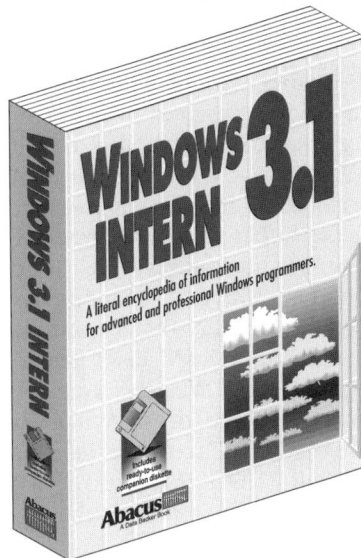

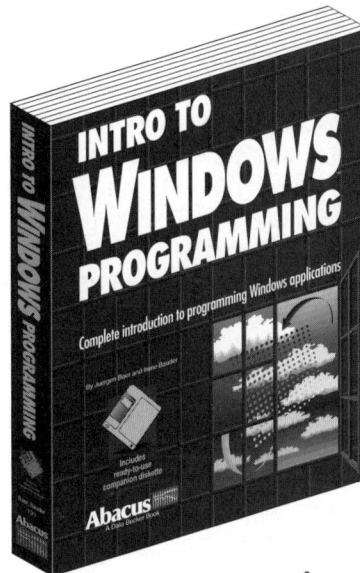

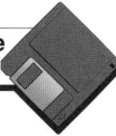

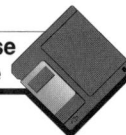

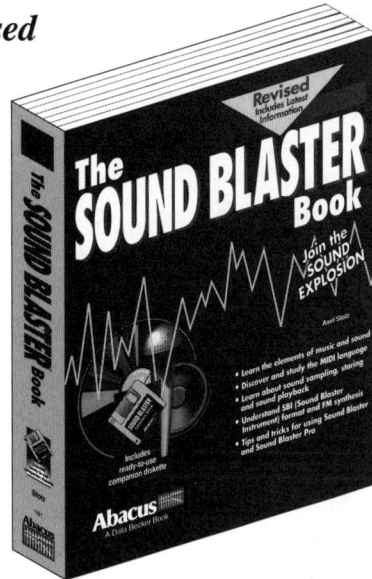

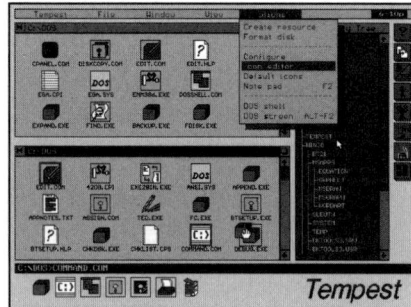